BELOVED COMMUNITY

The Sisterhood of Homeless Women in Poetry

A W•H•E•E•L ANTHOLOGY

Whit Press

Seattle, Washington • Jackson Hole, Wyoming • www.WhitPress.org

Book design by Tracy Lamb
Cover photo Eva Serrabassa, iStockPhoto.com

Published by
Whit Press
1634 Eleventh Avenue
Seattle, WA 98122
www.WhitPress.org

ISBN 978-0-9720205-5-8
Library of Congress Control Number: 2007920720

 Whit Press *Special thanks to ...*

Whit Press books are made possible in major part by the generous support of Nancy Nordhoff,
Sherri Ontjes, Margot Snowdon, Lynn Garvey, Jill McKinstry, Moira and Ken Mumma,
Linden Ontjes, Dr. Arthur Whiteley, Amal Sedkey-Winter, our individual contributors
and the following foundations and organizations:

• The Helen B. Whiteley Center, University of Washington, Friday Harbor
• The Seattle Foundation
• Seattle Office of Arts & Cultural Affairs
• The Breneman-Jaech Foundation
• The Hill-Snowdon Foundation
• Hedgebrook Retreat for Women Writers

For you all, our most heartfelt thanks and gratitude.

THE WHEEL MISSION STATEMENT

The Women's Housing, Equality and Enhancement League is a non-profit and non-hierarchical group of homeless and formerly homeless women working on ending homelessness for women. WHEEL is all about empowerment and action.

WHEEL is the women-only, women-concerned sister organization to SHARE (Seattle Housing and Resource Effort). Both WHEEL and SHARE provide self-managed shelters — including Tent Cities.

WHEEL works to get women out of the places where they have been hiding, recognize each woman as an individual and involve women in the process of improving programs and creating new programs for their own needs.

WHEEL's goals are to give voice and leadership to homeless women, to organize campaigns around increased services and safety for women, and to develop and support self-managed shelters.

ACKNOWLEDGMENTS

We at WHEEL extend heartfelt acknowledgements:

To Claudia Mauro and any and all at Whit Press
and other organizations who have helped
make this book possible.

To those who have helped put out our annual chapbooks,
from which these poems were taken:
Real Change,
Angeline's Day Center,
The Church of Mary Magdalene / Mary's Place,
SHARE,
Golem Copy Center,
YWCA.

And to all the poets who've courageously
shared their words and experiences with us.

Thank you.

INTRODUCTION

WHEEL (the Women's Housing, Equality and Enhancement League) is a scrappy little grassroots organizing effort of homeless and formerly homeless women in Seattle, Washington. Founded in 1993 by a group of courageous women, WHEEL is unique in the United States, and has been responsible for many great victories that have increased the safety, dignity and survival of homeless women in our city.

I've been WHEEL's Organizer since 1995. The beauty of WHEEL is that homeless and formerly homeless members are the voice, the vote, and the public face of the organization. Women involved with WHEEL define themselves, speak for themselves, and make their own decisions. It is not my role to tell you who the individual women of WHEEL are: you'll have to meet them, work with them, or read the poems collected in this anthology, published with our gratitude by Whit Press.

I *can* tell you what the women of WHEEL have done: defied all odds, assumptions and expectations about what homeless women working together can accomplish. When WHEEL started, no one thought homeless women could organize. They thought homeless people could never get beyond their basic need for survival in order to work toward a greater good. They thought homeless people were too isolated to work together in community. They thought homeless women in particular were too broken to be leaders in their community—too compromised and beaten down to speak truth to power.

They were wrong.

The women of WHEEL have been responsible for the development of several emergency shelters in Seattle that have saved countless lives. WHEEL has worked with developers to create housing programs that give dignity back to women who have been homeless for a long time. WHEEL has led the struggle, with their co-ed partner organization, SHARE (Seattle Housing and Resource Effort), to set up and support two controversial and wonderful Tent Cities. WHEEL women have started a homeless-led **Women in Black** movement, holding public vigils to remember and honor homeless people who die on the streets of Seattle/King County, and are well on the way toward building a public memorial. WHEEL women run their own education and arts center, publish a street newsletter, and do things as simple as making sandwiches every week to hand out to people who are hungry.

WHEEL women rally, march, and raise banners. They have staged "die-ins" on the steps of City Hall, held press conferences, and have met with every Mayor of Seattle for the past 14 years.

WHEEL also continues to sponsor yearly civic gatherings, called Homeless Women's Forums, inviting politicians, bureaucrats, social service providers, religious leaders, and ordinary citizens to hear their stories, celebrate their victories, and join with them to end homelessness. In conjunction with these yearly Forums, WHEEL women publish their own slim volume of poetry. Many of the poems in this anthology were first published in these books.

I can also give you a few snapshots of WHEEL poets and leaders. Some are in this book. Some just live on in our memories. There's Marion Sue Fischer, with a wild gleam in her eye, climbing onto a dumpster behind the large city shelter to shout out her poetry and plead for the powers that be to move the shelter entrance out of a dangerous alley and onto "beautiful sunlit Third Avenue."

There's Anitra Freeman, getting lost in blackberry brambles of a greenbelt at 3 AM, trying to find Tent City in order to get arrested with her compatriots for setting up an outdoor shelter on public land.

There's Cynthia Ozimek, wearing a chef's hat and dragging a large suitcase across a Methodist Church altar to comically make a point about bad shelter food and fashionable bag lady baggage to the hundreds of church folks gathered to hear her.

There's Carol, who lived in her car in the wealthy suburbs for two years after she became homeless, buying lunch for everyone at the Women's Empowerment Center with the first paycheck from her new job, her first job in years.

There's group after group of women pooling their pennies in order to buy flowers to adorn the steps of the Justice Center where they stand Women in Black vigils for the dead. There's woman after woman trudging up to the food bank to get staples in order to prepare delicious meals to share with her sisters.

And finally, what I can tell is the feeling that suffuses all of WHEEL's work. It is a feeling of great love. *"At the risk of seeming ridiculous, let me say that the true revolutionary is guided by great feelings of love,"* said Che Guevara. The women of WHEEL show their love for one another over and over again. I have been the recipient of this love many times. The revolution WHEEL started and continues to build has been a revolution of the heart, completely.

Every day, the experience of living with, working with, struggling with and writing with homeless women reminds me of one of Raymond Carver's last poems, "Late Fragment:"

> *And did you get what*
> *you wanted from this life, even so?*
> *I did.*
> *And what did you want?*
> *To call myself beloved, to feel myself*
> *beloved on the earth.*

The women of WHEEL haven't worked together or written poetry in order to be loved. They've done it to be seen, and known, and to make a DIFFERENCE.

I have loved every minute of my work with WHEEL, and I have loved every woman who is a part of this unique group. I defy you to meet them, read their poems, and not love them too.

— *Michele Marchand*

IN MEMORIAM
by Anitra L. Freeman

I am not resigned to the shutting away of loving hearts in the hard ground.
—Edna St. Vincent Millay, "Dirge without Music"

The list of names in this **In Memoriam** section were all friends of ours; women who had been homeless, who died in the past 14 years. They all had value to our community. They all were loved. Even though sometimes their death went unnoticed by the rest of the world, *we* noticed. We grieve their passing, still.

It feels like being robbed, when someone you love dies. In your gut, it feels *unfair*.

People become landmarks in our lives. We, especially we women, define ourselves by relationships. Nothing we love can be lost. It should be impossible. We will not allow it.

This is true for both housed and homeless people, but once you've been stripped of most of your material possessions, as homeless people are, the robbery of losing a loved one means you have less to cushion that loss. Emotions are rawer, and the hurt cuts deeper. Sometimes when you're homeless, the only possession you have is your friend.

When I became homeless in 1995, I discovered an "invisible side of the street." It appalled me, in the first nights I spent in a homeless shelter, to find women in their 60s sleeping on the concrete floor of a church basement, with one thin rubber mat and two army blankets. I didn't know we let that happen in our country.

I remember a small, bent woman stomping into the shelter kitchen with her walker, *demanding* to be allowed to wash her own dishes. I remember small, scrappy Pearl, up on a podium in the winter wind, *demanding* shelter for all of Seattle's women. Perhaps as we get older, it becomes clearer: above all material needs, what we need, to stay human, is our human dignity. And each other.

We have had our courageous young people, too — and lost them. I remember Anita Williams, and the Native American poem, *All Is a Circle Within Us*, that she brought to our writing group. I didn't realize who it was until her death was announced. "Anita Williams" is not evocative of First Nations. Then someone mentioned the poem. Then I saw her there, reading it.

When we decided to stand **Women In Black** vigils for homeless people who died outside, or by violence in King County. The first person we stood vigil for was Debbie Cashio. I didn't recognize her name at first either, until I saw her photograph. Then I remembered her standing in the early morning gathering on the sidewalk in front of Angeline's Day Center. In my memory, I see her giving another woman a cigarette. She is described as generous by those who knew her much better than I did. So many of the people we stand vigils for are described by their friends as generous.

One person whose generosity I knew firsthand was Cynthia Ozimek. Not generous as in giving me cigarettes (I don't smoke) or anything else material. She was generous with her heart, with her mind, with her poetry. She became a landmark in my soul, and in many others.

Cynthia died in 2005. We had more deaths that year in our homeless community in Seattle than ever before. We had more suicides than we had ever seen before, including our dear Dinah Lane. We had more homicides. At the announcement of Cynthia's death, a woman cried, "*What is happening to my sisters?*" One woman at Cynthia's memorial service described how often and how eloquently Cynthia had spoken up for the plight of homeless women and simple human justice, and asked, "*Who will speak for us now?*"

And the next speaker answered, "We all will." We must all speak for each other.

The numbers of homeless people have kept rising; and the numbers without shelter, the numbers killed by violence, the numbers despairing to the point of suicide, have also kept rising. In 2005 we stood vigil for a tragic record of 56 homeless people who died outside or by violence in King County; in 2006 we had a terrible new record of 59.

But we also have an increasing number of women standing up, standing together, speaking out, working for better.

When homeless women remember other homeless women, it is not often with mementoes. We seldom have an inheritance of garden, house, favorite chair, or even a pair of shoes. I tried to plant a tree in a tub for my friend Colette Fleming, after her memorial service, but I couldn't keep it going.

We remember each other in sharing what our friends have written, and in writing about them; as we do here, in this book. We stand our **Women In Black** vigils, and work for a permanent Place of Remembrance where perhaps there will be names carved in stone, and green plants that keep on growing. And we remember by continuing the work, to bring all women inside: into shelter, into dignity, into community, into relationships, into remembrance.

Each time we share names and our beloved memories, we are building up the landmarks of our beloved community. And finally, I realize, it is true.

Nothing we love is ever lost.

IN MEMORIAM

Since 2000, WHEEL has held a **"Women in Black"** *vigil in front of City Hall every time a homeless woman is found dead outside or by violence in King County. These are the names of the women, our sisters, among the 230 that we have stood for so far.*

Debbie Cashio, 40 — murdered by unknown method, May 2000 (7th & Jackson)

Robin Langston, 27 — stabbed, September 2000 (Belltown)

Melissa Marshall, 36 — stabbed, August 2001 (Kent)

Kathy Bowman, 35 — unknown cause of death, August 2001 (1st Avenue)

Rae Ann Champaco, 30 — stabbed, January 2001 (Freeway Park)

Kelly Rhae Craft, 44 — stomped to death, July 2002 (Kent)

Christine Doty, 38 — run over by train, January 2003 (Auburn)

Betty Diller — unknown cause of death, June 2003 (10th & Spruce)

Sandra Lee Smiscon, 45 — shot, July 2003 (4th & Yesler)

Julie Ann Sterling, 46 — strangled, August 2003 (near Seward Park)

Rosanna Koontz, 51 — unknown cause of death, September 2003 (Boren & Pike)

Deborah Estrada, 39 — unknown cause of death, January 2004 (Auburn)

Delores Beamon, 54 — unknown cause of death, January 2004 (Capitol Hill)

Dori Cordova, 31 — shot, May 2004 (Miller Community Center)

Yvetta Gene Krauss, 42 — unknown cause, September 2004 (SW 98th & 16th SW)

Maria McQuakay, 29 — suicide, October 2004 (the Jungle)

Jackie Ortega — brain aneurysm, November 2004 (Harborview)

Renee William, 51 — unknown cause of death, November 2004

Jayme Engelson, 21 — suicide by train, November 2004 (Auburn)

Alvena Whiteplume, 59 — burned to death, December 2004 (Frink Park)

Rhonda Starr, 39 — unknown cause of death, January 2005 (Rainier Valley)

Dinah Lane, 53 — suicide, January 2005 (4th & Lenora)

Susan Eileen Redhorn, 51 — sepsis, May 2005 (Waterfront)

Vanessa Murray Jones, 51 — stroke, June 2005

Sally Ann Howard, 53 — unknown cause of death, August 2005 (2nd & Yesler)

Cynthia Lee Ozimek, 45 — pneumonia, August 2005

Davina Garrison, 42 — murdered by unknown method and set on fire, November 2005 (under Alaskan Way viaduct)

Cindi Colleen Attison, 33 — hit by car, November 2005 (NE 70th & Roosevelt)

Sarah Gregory, 24 — heroin overdose, December 2005 (Ballard)

Irene Giguerre, 50 — blunt force injury, cause unknown, March 2006 (Aurora Ave. N)

Tonya "Sonshine" Smith, 47 — stabbed, June 2006 (10th & S. Weller)

Melissa Davis, 23 — stabbed, September 2006 (Courthouse Park)

THE WHEEL ANTHOLOGY SELECTIONS

CREDO

We each have a wise and a passionate heart, with a shell built around it to keep it from breaking that keeps it from living.

The spiritual path is breaking that shell and unfolding that heart.

To love truly is not to love others more, or to love self more, or even to love God more, but to love life more; to love the life of the heart more than the life of the shell.

The greatest act of love is to do what you fear to do, to say what you fear to say, to think what you fear to think, and to feel what you fear to feel.

The greatest act of wisdom is to live without easy answers, or even without answers at all, in order to live with more heart.

—Anitra L. Freeman

DEDICATION

to all of our sisters who have been homeless

BELOVED COMMUNITY

The Sisterhood of Homeless Women in Poetry

ODE TO POETRY

They tell me this is a book of poetry.
Write poetry, my friend, I hear them say.
I ask myself of my poetic side,
can I articulate in verse that rhymes?
Trained as I am in scientific lore, however,
never assisted me in explaining the intricacies
of the illusions I bore.

Only poetry commands the language I seek,
to put into a framework the visions
that flow through me at any given time.
Slowly, slowly through poetry will I unwind.
I will pick the strands of creative flow and
put the illness down. By the way,
Schizophrenia was all science ever found.

—*Sheryl Barlia*

TRENDS OF SOCIETY

I tried real hard to be a follower
Like my mother said all young ladies should be
I learned to cook and sew and dress the part
Even though the world kept calling out to me
I followed the trends of society

Now I was expected to get married
Like my mother said all young ladies should be
So I agreed to the first man that asked
Even though my heart longed for the world to see
I followed the trend of society

It didn't take long to become pregnant
Like my mother said married ladies should be
So I stayed at home raising three children
But the walls started closing in around me
I followed the trends of society

I tried real hard to be a follower
Like my mother said married ladies should be
I had his money but never his love
I had to walk away and set myself free
Ignoring the trends of society

I was not meant to be a follower
Like my mother had convinced me I should be
I was meant to go out and face the world
And become all that I can possibly be
Not follow the trends of society

Here I am finally seeing the world
A world that trend-followers will never see
Right or wrong they keep following the crowds
Not me, I ride the winds that helped set me free
To hell with the trends of society

—*Debbie Bessette*

OUTREACH

For months I watched you, you with your warm clothes and big smiles. You always stopped me on the street to say, "Hello! How are you, today?" And I'd duck my head and mumble something back, standing on one foot, trying to keep the other warm.

You always looked so happy. You told me I'd be happy, too, if I'd come to your church and be saved like you. I figured you know what you were talking about; you were always so happy. You had warm clothes and you never looked hungry. I wanted that, too, so I went to your meeting. I sat with you and all your friends. I tried to sing your songs. I liked that one about all of us being one in the spirit. And you and your friends sat down with me and asked, would I like to be saved, too? I couldn't get my voice to work, so I just nodded. But when you said, Pray after me, I got the words out, all of them. I said them right, right after you.

I started to cry. You all smiled and nodded and left me alone, up there in the church. I waited and waited for something to happen. I waited for anything to happen. I didn't know how long it was supposed to take to be saved, so I just sat and listened to my stomach grumbling.

And you left me there, still waiting for something to happen. I was feeling awfully hollow inside.

When the lights in the church went off, I tried to find someone, but the room we sang in was all locked up, and I didn't hear anyone laughing or singing anywhere, anymore. You had all gone. It's cold outside. It's a long way home from your church. My cheeks still burn where the tears sort of froze on them. And, I'm still hungry. I guess that doesn't matter so much as the aching, hollow feeling inside me. I didn't really mind walking home, either. I just wish somebody'd tell me what went wrong.

Didn't I wait long enough? I know I don't sing too good, but I said the prayer right, and I can learn the songs. I'd practice ... and I'd go to the meetings and to church. I promise! Come back, someone! I'm all alone. Somebody, please come back and tell me why He didn't want to save me. I'm waiting ...

—*Elizabeth Wicker Bennefield*

A PRAYER FOR TENT VILLAGE

Father God in Heaven
In the mighty name of Jesus:
Forgive my sins, seen and unseen:

Thou said Love thy neighbor.
Thou said Bless our enemies.
Thou said Ask:

We ask Thee, Lord, to bless Tent City,
Lord, the people of the land,
the people You have chosen to be out in the elements:

Let us all Remember
the battle is the Lord's,

that You know and will bless the ones in authority
to be understanding, yet firm in courage.

We thank Thee,
for what You are doing.
and about to do,
in Jesus's name.

—Penny Boggs

CHILDREN

Children
playing, loud
on a swing
Push me
Higher

—Cynthia Burton

HAIKU

food, noise, prayers, conflict
and inspiration
all found at Mary's Place

—*Carol C.*

KAREN (1951-1995)

If you die on me
I will spit
on your grave
to make
the weeds grow.

Who will I call
at 5 a.m.?
Who will tell me
to take my medicine?
Who will call me a little twit;
give me her cat
to take care of?
Who will refuse
to buy my painting
because I have borrowed too much?

Who will I stay with all night and talk
till morning
about the Army
and Marine Corps;
our fathers
and step-fathers
touching us;
our first loves;
the men we are with now;
the time we met on the mental ward
and danced in pajamas
and striped robes,
on the V.A. patio,
while the other patients played
Bingo and the American Legion
members served cookies
and coffee with caffeine,

the time we lived together
on 18th St. when you moved
all the furniture
and we drank White Russians
on the porch;
the second-hand book stores
we browsed where cats curled
on couches or stared
out store-front windows,
the hats that make you look like a cow girl
with dangling earrings?

Karen, who will I talk to
if not to you?

—*Crysta Casey*

MAN OVERBOARD

Sweat dampens the pillow case,
wets the sheets. He is caught
in a bad dream, being
a gunner on a Navy ship
off the shores of Vietnam.
A little box. The only
escape is overboard.
He doesn't know how
to swim. A girlfriend
tried to teach him once
in Spain, but he was too
afraid of water.
Now, he's caught in the cracks
of the system, on Welfare,
Social Security, and V.A. Pension
pending, deep depression and a desire
to drown in Puget Sound.
He surfs couches, as he calls it,
or borrows a spare bedroom.
He is tempted to take
the first $6 an hour job
that comes along, but his art calls.

The shadow on a woman's thigh,
her dark crotch, legs spread as she lies
on the bed, her eyes a mystery
of grown children, lost lovers, dreams
and shaky hopes for an uncertain future.
Her hair graces her forehead
in wisps. He loves to paint
all this. This is it
when he isn't wandering
the sidewalks, talking
to a former crack addict who sells

the homeless paper outside Starbucks.
He thinks she is a sixteen year old
runaway. She turns out to be
22, knows things. He would buy her
coffee, but his pocket has three
pennies. He would throw these
in the fountain in front of the insurance
building on Sixth Avenue, make wishes
for some other homeless person to wade in
and pick out. He worries she has gone
back, back to her crack friends
when he doesn't see her with her pile of papers for two weeks.

He likes looking at people:
fat bodies, skinny bodies,
sagging breasts and butts.
Firm tits, tips cold from lying
exposed on a blanket, perhaps
in an open burgundy robe ...
he is dreaming. He isn't watching
the traffic. He isn't even
aware that he's crossing
the street. He doesn't care
if the cars keep coming.
He hears the bell
that rings in his ear
to let the blind know it's safe to cross
and wonders what round it is
from his boxing days.
He has no sense of direction, he is lost again.
He knows only that if he finds
the water he will know
where West is. If he doesn't jump
in this time, he may wind
his way home.

—*Crysta Casey*

30

SELF-PORTRAIT

A self-portrait hangs
above him sleeping
restlessly on the mattress.
His legs kick like a horse's
pawing the dirt, clump, clump,
tangled in a blue quilt.
In the portrait, his face glows orange,
the background purple,
the complimentary colors
of a sunset in Vietnam,
but the eyes, the eyes
(and the heart he painted
black below the left breast),
the eyes suffer the sorrow
of a drafted man
who didn't want to kill
and later met the refugees,
strung electric wire
for the relatives of those
he bombed. His legs run away
with his dreams, tangled
in the blue quilt of night.

I woke once to my husband
bare-ass naked on all fours,
pawing the wooden floor
with his bowie knife.
I called him
out of sleep as he fought
the dreamed enemy
and later, fully awake,
he walked into the woods
with a bottle of whiskey
and all his pills.

After three months, a father
and his son were looking
for fossils and found his bones.

My lover's eyes
are closed tonight
beneath blankets,
and though he is not at peace
I will let him sleep.

—*Crysta Casey*

38° AND RAINING

God, it's cold
Oh, so terribly cold
It's as if every bone in my body
     Feels
As if it were made of stainless steel
My toes are numb
I have no clean socks
And the holes in the bottoms
of my shoes have invited the rain
     To drain
Me of any comfort

I am contorted by the cold.
My fingers curl into claws
     And it hurts
To hold onto my meager belongings
     Everything aches
It's so wet and cold
And now, the winds
Whipping the world around, around me
     Into a devil's frenzy
I am a walking zombie
I would be warmer in a grave ...
... with earth around me ...

Oh God, please deliver me.
I can spell hypothermia.
I can die from it, too.
All the shelters are full.
     What am I to do?
Keep moving, or curl up in a doorway?
I have no one left to depend on, but you.

—Catherine M. Condeff

DID YOU HEAR THAT?

This was written due to memories of
sleeping in a downtown stairwell and hanging
out in the Metro underground tunnel.

I'll never forget it
I was surrounded by cement
And I burst out
      with a pent-up
      built-up
      monstrous scream

So loud
It echoed off the walls
So full of anguish ...
      the echoes lingered in my ears
And then I wept
      bitter tears
      from an empty heart
      with a voice
      that was now, barely there

No one came by
      the walls served as silent sentinels
      In the war that I had lost. ..
      ... Or so it seemed

I screamed
      again.
This time, my jaw yawned wide
      like a python about to devour
      the minutes that had to have been hours
Yet this scream was a silent scream.
      It erupted from the basement
      floor of my soul.

Angels in heaven
were awakened by the agony
They heard.
Even a few of those in hell
        cocked their heads
        for a moment, and paused to ... listen.

Then it was Back to Business
(This is nothing new to them)

Once, I said to another, I said,
"I have two guardian angels — because one has to rest
while the other angel is on duty."
And then I laughed.

Yet, now I know.
There must be two.
And the one who was sleeping
Was paid for overtime later
For when that silent scream
Was heard by him (or her)
he (or she)
had no shoes to grab, yet
He (she) came running.

—*Catherine M. Condeff*

PRACTICE MAKES PERFECT

If practice makes perfect,
Then I'm still on that road
Mile after mile after mile·
And I've still got a long ways to go
Practicing, baby, practicing
Got to get it right
Don't always work in the daytime
Don't always sleep at night

If practice makes perfect, then really
I thought I'd have it down by now
Sometimes feeling like a social reject
Sometimes being the circus clown
But I gotta keep on practicing
Got to get it straight
Doubt I'll get there early
But I'll be damned if I'm too late

     There's a hole in my shoe
     But I gotta keep on walkin'
     They're not listening to you,
     But still, you keep on talkin'
     The suffering we've been through
     Weighs a humongous ton
     But it's not a matter of win or lose
     It's the way the race is run

—*Catherine Condeff*

(REMEMBERING)
WHAT IT'S LIKE

I HAVE TO BE STRONG
I HAVE NO CHOICE
My heart is a muscle
My soul has a voice

There is not time for weakness
Can't risk being wrong
Hope is the rope I've clung to so long

My faith mustn't waver
One slip, and I go down
down to death~ Sister Death wears
A weighty weathered gown.

So, it's time to flex my heart
And sing with all my soul
Lest the angels cannot find me
In this slick, cement hellhole
        to some, it's just a city
They fly in, they pay for neon, do their gig
And out they go
But I sleep and breathe on these sidewalks
And dig through the things they throw

Away, — Oh, get up, self
Get moving you — you Lazarus
Let's belong to somewhere else
I'm hoping I can get here by myself
Carry on, like a leper without lesions
And pray that the faith and the love will soon kick in

I'm not letting the devil have me
This city will not do me in.

Let's find some warmth in a human smile
Let's gain some green from a tree
Let's not our souls surrender
      to this vain insanity

Instead, let's have a picnic
We'll try to get some foodbank food
And we'll share it with the birds
And maybe make a friend or two

Just a little further
Tomorrow's a whole 'nother deck of cards
And maybe these folks won't turn me in
If I borrow for awhile their yards.

—*Catherine M. Condeff*

GROUND ZERO

I've learned Life is too short —
to disrespect another human's dignity.

In recognizing this, I became able.
Able to respond to the hardships I,
and many of us, face, day in and day out.

I learned to utilize the many resources that
the wonderful city of Seattle has to offer.

I found strength and courage I didn't know I possessed.
I received help and direction, and a way out of my own
    way.
I want to thank all my sisters for every little thing good that
    is now.

—Janice Connelly

CUPID

Cupid in my heart,
Its arrow hid.
Excite love that
Reality forbid.
Ever-throbbing, over-
Flowing, burst my
Heart its lid.
Melt into a tale, tepid
Yet, vivid.

—*Mary Cutler*

A TRIBUTE

The following tribute was written in memory of a thirty-nine year old homeless woman who died of three stab wounds to the chest. She died in Yesler Park one night this past June 1992.

Her death was an act of violence. Among the homeless her senseless death resulted in a mixture of feelings, anger, fear, hopelessness and vulnerability. It left so many unanswered questions for those on the streets, especially; "Why did she have to die so needlessly?"

Those who knew and loved her, miss her laughter and her willingness to share the little she had with those who had even less.

The following poem was written for her by her friend Jean. It is a loving tribute to her life and the effect it had on those around her.

ANNA

I lost a Friend today
She wasn't important except to Me.
She left a small Estate.
Something else you can't see.
I miss her and her joy and pain
I'll think about her often
I hate the way she died.
Alone on the ground
With no one to let her know
She wasn't alone.

—*Jean Dawson*

SHOW ME SHELTER

Where do I go when the shelters are full?
No one has a place for me.
The alleys are dangerous,
a doorway so cold!

Maybe I'll sleep in a cardboard box.

When will someone give us more space?
How can I get a decent job
when no one has rooms?
A shelter seems to help only those with special needs,
but no room for me.

Maybe I'll sleep in a cardboard box.

A roof and a bed, and a place to bathe
just so I can go to work.
Without a place to get clean
I cannot get ahead.

Maybe I'll sleep in a cardboard box.

Please help me enjoy
all that you have.
A place of warmth
and safety from the danger outside.

Maybe I'll sleep in a cardboard box.

Please understand
I want the same things as you.
A job, a safe home,
and maybe somebody who cares.

—*Betty E.*

BAG LADY FASHION UPDATE

Plop a bonnet on your head and get those ivories fixed! Old Sol is peeping through the clouds and its time to wear a smile. Dump your plastic bags and replace them with colorful cottons. Also, delicate sandals are in, and help dispel winter's mildew! This Spring's colors are pink, yellow, orange and blue! Don't be mean to Mr. Bumblebee, Ladies. He loves the look, too!

—Carol Fallman

OVERCOMING THE FEAR

Apprehension and depression seemed to persist. "Come on, get your head together," I thought. "You should be glad, thankful. This is a new beginning, a chance to succeed, or at least have some privacy and a place of my own again, finally.

"You were lucky." My thoughts turned to the other ladies left in the shelter. You just don't realize what you've given up in those places. It's dehumanizing, rough. I thought I could handle it, but now I know I'd touched the hurt way down inside on top of the hurt pile I've accumulated.

God, why is life so complicated, unjust? Seems in a country like this a person should at least have a place to live.

Wonder how long the insecure and fearful feeling will last. Spent most of the money I'd saved, which wasn't much on $339 a month. The floors were hard linoleum, gray, and there were no drapes. Need so many more things, sure hope my check arrives OK. Damn, it's so expensive just to pick up a few necessary items for a small apartment. Bet it cost twice as much now as a year ago. I know now I can't ever live like that again. It's left me with a mark that can't be erased, maybe in time ...

I wish everyone at Second and Cherry had found a place. I need to stay in touch. Makes me feel sad.

—*Carol Fallman*

PERCEPTIONS

Leaves are strewn about the sidewalks
     In many different hues
One falls just now from a tree in front of me
As I walk along, going nowhere

The rain falls and my hat gets soggy
My face is wet, and my feet are cold
I acknowledge the beauty I would see all around
     If I still had a home
I would choose to stay inside
     on a day like this
Standing in from of my blazing fireplace
     Arms outstretched
Contented, toasty and dry.

—DeAnn Ferguson

AFRICAN QUEEN

WE brought her over
        from Africa
in the (intolerable)
        holds of slave ships

        (fast-forward)

She is STILL a QUEEN,
in her jazzy,
        Regal
    and colorful
        Rags,

Rolling her
        elegant Luis Vuitton
Suitcase
        behind her,

ON
the
streets
        of Seattle,

Mumbling Royal
        Curses
            jokes
    and blessings,
to ME
Her friend

(... AND, perhaps,
to her GOD ...)

Her Power UNDIMINISHED,
her Mind
Departs the Amarikan construct

Which has SO VICIOUSLY
        ABUSED her,

Coming through,
Beautiful and strong,
With the heady heat
Of Another Land

      I tried being
Her Slave, for a time
(I felt I owed it to her ...)

Her Imperial Grandness
      Preceding me,
As I trailed her suitcase
      behind

OR,

Her arm linked
in mine,
for Support
      (She tires easily, now
      in her 70's ...)

BUT,

If there appeared
Someone she knew,
She carried
Her own luggage,

OR,

Unlinked her arm ...

Her Beauty matched
ONLY
by her Dignity ...

—*Marion Sue Fischer*

AM I THERE YET?

In/The/Silence
I have visions

Dinner turns into breakfast
In this place of
NO TIME

I
find
my
Peace

(learn to speak
to/the/Silence ...)

—Marion Sue Fischer

CLOUDING

These Old People:
My neighbors

(Am I one of them?)

Have cataract surgery
The way I take-a-drink
and
Both for the same reason:
To CLOUD the "doors of perception ... "

    them: to cloud INWARD perception
    me: to cloud OUTWARD perception

TOO MUCH CLARITY
      and
You're
      NAKED-IN-THE-SUN

—Marion Sue Fischer

FAITH

BEAUTY
Like Life, itself

is persistent

And
Will (eventually) OVERCOME

The ugliness
Man has perpetrated

Upon/the/Earth

—Marion Sue Fischer

HEALING

We carry our History
with us

in our Minds
in our muscles
in our Blood
... in our very BONES

It colors
the way We See
and feel
the way we react
and interact

... our very Lives

There IS relief
There CAN be release
There can be Healing

I believe

and

Only YOU know
The Way

... for YOU

—*Marion Sue Fischer*

OF J

She saves her precious papers
(why <u>precious</u> known only
   to herself ...)
TRUNDLES them around
 six bags
 in tandem,
Corner-to-corner
 to Street

On the Streets—

Cross back to get
 the last two,
Circle the light pole
 five times

RITUAL all
 her OWN

Who am <u>I</u> to
 SAY,
Scribbling compulsively
Felling trees with every
 Pen/stroke,

The VALUE of
HOW
she
spends
HER

Life ...

—*Marion Sue Fischer*

ON OUR CITY STREETS

Perhaps

She simply has no tears
Left
To
          Cry/for/herself

Lying on a sidewalk
Her face BROKEN
Bleeding like a wild animal
Saying "I'm okay!"

On/our/city/streets....

Who <u>did</u> this to her?
this woman I have
shared shelter with,
broken bread with?

Who COULD have
<u>Done</u> this to her?
What offense so dire
To provoke this assault?

A young woman-of-the-streets
Lying on a sidewalk;
Bloody-faced, bloody-headed
Saying "I'm okay!"
Dry-eyed, with confidence
or is it the energy of anguish?
Startled by our concern

On/our/city/streets....

She asks for no help
Has she ever tried
Asking/for/help?
Has she ever gotten any?

Has it left her here?

...lying on a sidewalk
Her clothes torn and soiled
Bloody-headed, dry-eyed
...and alone...?

On/our/city/streets....

Was she once
Her Mother's Little Darling?
Her Father's gleam-in-the-eye?
Did she laugh and play
Like other girls?

What led her here?
Has she CHOSEN this path?

...lying on a sidewalk
On our city streets
Bloody-faced, dry-eyed
        and alone
Saying "I'M okay!"

—*Marion Sue Fischer*

RECOURSE FOR WOMEN

I

Can we get
        SOME fuckin' Recourse
for our BLASTED minds,
        our Blasted LIVES??

Can we HAVE
        Some FUCKIN' Recourse
        for our abandonment
        by our society,
        families,
        our CHILDREN,
        friends,
        our MEN
        our Selves,
        our World,
if NOT our GOD ...

II

... Asking little
        if ANYTHING,
down to Basics,
we get
        NOTHING
(... oh, a frown or a smile ...)

III

Was it our FAULT
        to
        demand so
        Little,
in a society
        BUILT ON GREED,

Packaging itself in
the "Giant Economy Size,"
"CHEAPER by the Dozen,"
"BUY ten, GET ONE 'FREE.'"

IV

Dressing ARTFULLY
LIVING Artfully
        on Cough Drops,
                showers and
        medication,
        CIGARETTES,
Garbage,
                Free Meals
And FAITH

... FOR NO REASON,
        Apparent failures,
OPTING, for the Good of
                ALL

to Live in
        Our
                OWN World

... since there is/was
        NO PLACE for
        us
        in
        "YOURS,"

V

JOIN US
        in
        Love.
(it is NOT only MONEY we ALL need ...)

—*Marion Sue Fischer*

REGRET

NOW

    would be a good time

for
    a partnership of
    deep friendship
    mutual affection
    and easy familiarity

Built up
    over
        many
            years

—Marion Sue Fischer

RONALD IS DEAD

No more
Letters or phone calls from Ronald

(Burden AND Gift
        as they were...)

Has he assumed/his/Spirit
        ...yet?

Is he (yet) ABLE to
        walk-thru-the-walls
        of this metal-clad God-forsaken trailer?

Will he slither thru
        the windows?
        the screens?

Will he WANT to visit me?
        (STILL Alive
        STILL waiting
        for some form of communication...)

Has he (FINALLY) ABANDONED me?
        (steadfast and loyal
        as he WAS to me
        throughout our MANY mutual lives...)

I wonder all this
As grad students
Dissect his
Hollow corpse
At U.C.L.A. Medical School

—*Marion Sue Fischer*

SAD TODAY ... : TO ROBIN

Sometimes

Sadness/wells/up

FILLS the emptiness

and

Gives me comfort

—*Marion Sue Fischer*

SEATTLE: "INVISIBLE" STREET WOMEN

People of Seattle:
You DON'T
      necessarily
Know
      WHO we ARE;

We are not all
      unkempt, toothless ladies
      carrying shopping bags;

We are not ALL
      mind-loss women
      of indeterminate age
      conversing with "unseen companions"
(tho' we would ALL, wouldn't we, prefer a COMPANION ...)

AND
these, too, are human beings ...

We MIGHT be
      the attractive, fashionably dressed, bright-eyed
      thirtyish female
      deep in a sense of Helplessness,
      living in a man-made world
      that has Engulfed, Overwhelmed her
      in Injustice,
      ... so forgive her, please, for forgetting how to
      "MAKE SENSE ... "

We MAY be
      thin, statuesque Black Lady, "pushing" 60,
      attired in a business suit
      (complete with flawless hose and black pumps,)
      looking like

your fourth-grade teacher ...
(perhaps she WAS ...)

We COULD BE
        the kindly-looking, pastel-hued,
        grandmotherly woman
        (she IS somebody's grandmother, you know ...)
        a worried look on her face,
        coughing from long hours spent on draughty city buses

        BECAUSE she <u>must</u> vacate her Shelter
        at 7:30, promptly, EVERY MORNING,
        not to return till 5:30 every EVENING ...
        (she is searching for her son ...)

We ARE People who
        shop in your stores,
        pass pleasantries with you, DAILY,
        enrich the texture of your city.

We TRY:
it is our <u>design</u>
to BE INVISIBLE,
to "fit in,"
... so your scorn will be reserved for <u>others</u>.

We "Keep up <u>Appearances</u>,"
tho' our lives
have lost the <u>coherence</u>,
      the <u>cohesion</u>,
You take for granted
      in your own ...

We invoke
a Mantle of Spirit to

GET
US
BY ...

ONE
MORE
DAY.

We LOOK like you;
we ARE you.

We do the <u>Best</u> we CAN
AND
deserve your RESPECT
which we <u>earn</u>

EVERY TIME
we SMILE.

  Thank you.

—*Marion Sue Fischer*

THE ROAD IS MADE IN THE WALKING: PALE TRAVELER

I am no machete-wielder
> In the jungle
> of life;

More like a ghost
> slipping unknown, unseen
> Amidst the underbrush,

… disturbing nothing …

And yet, there ARE those
> who will say

I have made
> a
> DIFFERENCE …

—Marion Sue Fischer

THESE CRAZY WOMEN: THE NERVE!!!

THESE WOMEN
Mucking up the
      Cogs of Our Machinery
Mucking ABOUT with the
      Machinery of our Society

Giving the Lie to
      Our Sanitized "Reality"

DISARRANGING our
      Convenience,
    our Expedience!

MELTING our
      Straight Lines
Curving our
      Right Angles

Slowing down
      Our Progress

      … on the Road to Extinction

—*Marion Sue Fischer*

THREE RECENT WIDOWS

It's taken something
　　out/of/us:

The end-of-Life care
　　　so DRAINING
The missing person
　　　companion-of-our-years
　　　　　　(no one to talk to
　　　　　　　　in the mornings
　　　　　　no one to fight with
　　　　　　　　to hear our complaints
　　　　　　　　　or the jokes
　　　　　　　　　　that-we-shared. . .)
The feeling of DEFEAT:
("death" won the battle. . .)

We <u>stoop</u> a little
　　　head down

We walk a
　　　little-more-infrequently

We cry more often

Our very Souls
　　　are more tender

Will God and Time
Heal the emptiness in our hearts?
　　　　　　　our homes?

Give us back
The spring-in-our-step
Our ready smiles
The joy in our lives

　　　?

—Marion Sue Fischer

TRUST

Thank you
For helping me FORGET
—for a time—

That I have seen
(what appeared to be)
Human beings

Look at me

The way a lion
Must look at
An antelope

—Marion Sue Fischer

UNTITLED

I thank Jesus
For my occasional
Clarity-in-the mornings

And, of course,
For the booze
To take the EDGE off

(COWARD THAT I AM)

Too cowardly to face
The world-of-man
As-I-am

I drink and smoke
To veil my Nature
(I have come to a painfully-earned
fear of people
AND their EVIL.)

—Marion Sue Fischer

UNTITLED

WILL I EVER
live somewhere

Where the hallways
don't betray evidence

of

Someone
Beyond/their/Breaking/Point?

—Marion Sue Fischer

WAITING TO GET IN

the Bearded White Man
SWAGGERING down the Alley
Between two lines of Homeless Women
thinks:

"Each ONE of them
Would rather be
      with ME
Than in the situation
      She's IN ... "

And you KNOW what??
      He's
      <u>wrong</u>:

Most of us have been THROUGH
      him, or
      some <u>version</u> of him,

And found his
      LIES unfathomable
    his Lies UNFATHOMABLE
    his Lies objectionable,
    his Lies ANATHEMA,

      and so,
here we are, in an Alley
Behind Noel House

Waiting
To
Get
IN.

—Marion Sue Fischer

A CHAMBER AND SOME MUSIC
(to Alice Wu)

—how there can be

                      nothing

    save this

barren wooden room

                    then one

    lone woman

             crosses

  to the

      center

  still   she   lifts

    a bow

            and sends it

coursing

      across

          strings

and from this sterile cavern

      sudden

        snap

            dragon

       fire

    cracker

and the coiled cobras

          spring—

—Ruth A. Fox

AN EYE FOR AN EYE LEAVES US ALL BLIND

lately we've all been hovering at the gorge
gouging each others' eyes and hiding
to deny the gap spreading
so we missed the second coming

      jesus is wandering through us
and she's not a pretty sight
doing the shuffle barefoot
rag blanket wrapped to ward off our chill
hair matted and eyes full of dread

night's advocate she needs
to disrupt our daily bread
as she sniffs out dumpsters
finding stale loaves and rank
fishes are not enough

silent knives dance so close
they nip her wrists and ankles
      and always moving she never rests
at any mean hearths
nor lays herself down on sterile beds

      instead she darts down alley shadows
seeking for specters
who can slip around sharp edges
to follow her dance
rapping on doors that long ago
lost the hope behind them

shepherded by street lamps
she shall want
and shall join in your communion
when your home also
crumbles off the pantry shelf

she shall not accept death as the solution this time

—*Ruth A. Fox*

PARA LA ESPERANZA
FOR HOPE

to Omar Castaneda who has let me know
since his death he is resting in peace

You fly	Tu voles
with the colors	con colores
of despair,	de dolor,
my choked	pajarito
little bird	ahogado
who has come	que viene
so far north.	de si afuera.
Come, listen	Ven, escouche
to your heart beat,	tu Corazon,
for although	para atudada
silent and	y sofocada,
suffocating,	todavia
Hope still	la esperanza
is blooming.	es en flor.
With the waves	Con las ondas
of her flowered	de esta agua
waters,	flociente,
I perfume myself,	yo mi perfumo
little bird.	pajarito.
You fly	Tu voles
in the night, yes?	en la noche,
Come	no? Ven,
nestle in	accurucar
the sunrise	en la sonrisa
of my	de mi nida
rosy nest.	rosada.

—Ruth A. Fox

DEBUNKING THE PROTESTANT WORK ETHIC

sleeping in on Saturday and reading
hold sway over updating my resume
and gathering friends
rates more than
folding strewn laundry

arms ache from lifting trays
and serving food for tossed bills
all left-over strength is spent
digging room in my own garden
I rebel
the pen drops unbidden
but bleeding ink stains hardwood floors
so I say this to you

sometimes that extra dollar
needs to be spent on coffee out
instead of saved for a sunny day
or paying debts or calling home
if you can have coffee money I want it too
your shit stinks and unwashed so would you
got a bathroom in this establishment?

—Ruth A. Fox

WE MASSES DON'T WANT TOFU

we masses don't want tofu thank you
we prefer pork chops and hearty beef stew
carrots cut thick will nourish the brew
but solo those tubers and sprouts just won't do
our bone-weary bodies need more than legumes
when there's one meal a day
and that day's work ain't through
hey poultry or seafood's okay by us too
but no more tofu please thank you

—Ruth A. Fox

WATER

More than wine
I am thinking about two women
sitting on the curb
Wet, even in ninety degrees
Because of the street-cleaner's hose
They haven't bought a drink
(bra straps showing)
From the establishment
They haven't bought the street
(skin, minority)
From the cleaners
But they do own the pavement
As witness to their experience
they've tasted it
The pavement
Through teeth blessed not to be broken
Don't ask me how I know
That we are all soaked
By the street cleaner's hose
Steamed on heated pavement
And drenched with
Water
More than wine
I am thinking how strong we
are not to be broken
Don't ask me how I know

—M. Noel Franklin

BEYOND THE TOMB

sentenced to death
for lack of truth
all of us
carry a cross.

when we all
fall
why do so many shun
the fallen?

we admire those who stand up for the truth
only when it is OUR truth

what awards do we give
  when those we look down on
act greater than we do?

a small kindness done
  outshines
a great kindness undone.
we can help one person a little
  if we cannot
save the world.

for there will be pain
and there will be death
but even the weakest can share warmth in the rain
and the grieving
can share comfort.

abandoned
despised
stripped of all dignity
we wait in mute suffering
for a better world;

curse God and die;

or ...

or ...

or ...

—Anitra L. Freeman

FEAR

I saw fire and thunder take three thousand people.
I don't even **know** three thousand people.
The same thing could kill **everyone I know**.

Fear makes my skin crawl now
When I hear of a madman holding weapons.
Make him go away.
Bomb his country until he loses power.

A woman in Iraq sits afraid.
Everyone she knows may die
Because of a madman she's never met.

—Anitra L. Freeman

FREEWAY PARK FEBRUARY 13, 2002

A woman who could not speak
was silenced here.

Doors that refuse to give a reason
lock shut on echoes.

Our black clothes whisper under the breath of sun
while candles pray on the sand
and the sage smoke dances.
The sun burns softly.
Little leaves weep down.

We are the only shout. We are a silent shout.

A rage of prayer
into tomorrow.

—Anitra L. Freeman

GOOD FRIDAY 2004

The Korean Memorial Wall
has faces in it.
They float into sight
like survivors float into notice.
They float out of sight
like survivors often do.

My husband, born in 1949,
calls himself a survivor of Korea.
Wes was one the day his daddy came back from war;
the first day of the child's four-month coma;
the day the Other Wes was born,
the Hawaiian brother
who keeps all the memories that could kill you.

The child of his loins
and the child of his violence—
are their faces floating in that wall?
Is his? The father who was killed;
the one who would have held his infant son
and laughed?

Bullets always take a part of you away.
I grew up with the scars in Daddy's back,
like craters rimmed with debris
from the splash of a meteor.
Holes in history.
So many things unseen
on the floor of craters.
That what fills Daddy's coffee cup
isn't coffee.
That the half-gallon of Gallo wine
is new each night.

There are things unheard, untouched, unthought, unfelt,
like what Daddy said that you didn't want him to say;
like what you wanted Daddy to say, that he never did.

Where in the wall
is the face left behind at Cho Sin Reservoir?
Where is mine?

A memorial for sacrifices
must honor all casualties,
doesn't it?

How many faces are there
in that wall?

—*Anitra L. Freeman*

GREGOR

I remember holding a small, warm body
He smelled like innocence and comfort

I remember our sister telling me
he was in jail somewhere in the Midwest
for a series of burglaries

Gregor was three the year he fell out of the cherry tree
He broke both arms and they kept him in the hospital a week
In a room with a little boy who'd lost an arm to a tractor
The paper printed a picture of the boy with one arm
feeding Gregor with a spoon

Gregor was five
the year Mother started screaming to her boyfriend
that the transformers outside the window
were going to explode
because demons were coming over the electric wires

I remember his small mute face in Dad's back room
owl eyes peeking out of neglected darkness
I remember his small pale face at Grandmother's house
but I can't remember the smell of innocence and comfort
any more

—*Anitra L. Freeman*

HEROINES

First I wanted to be
a bulldozer
the Little Red Engine Who Could
a flying unicorn.

Then I saw The Cowboy Queen.

I wanted two guns and a belt with tied-down holsters,
a cowboy hat hanging down my back
rawhide skirt and jacket, with fringe,
fancy-stitched gloves to leather-shield my knuckles
when I knocked bad guys flying,
and a lariat and a blacksnake whip
and a throwing knife strapped to my ankle.

I made them for myself
from the Emperor's clothes.
I camped out one afternoon in the attic
and almost got a fire started
before Mom smelled me out.

When I read more
I wanted to be Podkayne of Mars
or her second cousin: the one who
piloted my own spaceship,
foiled military takeovers of the galaxy,
cured the plague on suffering planets
and cooked gourmet meals from plankton.

In the really frustrating times
I dreamed of being an Amazon;
a strapping buxom redhead
who could swing a broadsword in each hand
and lay waste to ARMIES of idiots.

Now,
I've talked to city councils
and angry crowds
in 3-week old clothes and 3-day old hair.
I've told a doctor I'm depressed.
I've told a friend I lied.
And last night I walked eighteen blocks across Seattle
at 2:30 in the morning
safely
because I was not afraid.

I no longer want to be Red Sonja.

—*Anitra L. Freeman*

MANITOU

My mother's mothers walked on earth that spoke
in seed and sprout and flower, scented herb,
the ever present drum of tree and rock,
the year and season signaled by the moon.

Within the city walls my life is bound.
I find my friends, my healing mission here.
Earth's heart still beats, though muffled, in my bones;
a blood and breath I need for nourishment.

My skin is infinite and night and day
I feel both concrete and the softest leaf,
my lover's skin and stranger's acid eyes.
My heart digs for the life we share at root.

If I hear stars above the growling smog,
wind through the traffic's grumble, leaf's lone plaint
muffled in crowd's dull roar — then I will find
my loam and water under pavement's hold.

—*Anitra L. Freeman*

MAY 2003
Dedicated to She Who Must Not Be Named

They say hope springs eternal
in the human breast.
It is not so.
It is pushed up,
eternally.
That small green thread
contains heart's blood,
determined spirit; it rises from
the depths of principles we've grounded in
to push forward in the world
with our lives.
It is never too late
to raise it up again.

—Anitra L. Freeman

MOTHER'S DAY IN TENT CITY

For several years, WHEEL has made a tradition of serving a Mother's Day Brunch for homeless women. Mother's Day 2000 came during our Tent City 3 campaign. When we said that we would be unable to organize the brunch this year, OWL (the Older Women's League) came forward and brought brunch out to the tents.

Are we children on one side of midnight,
adults on the other?
Women until the kindling of one cell,
then instant mothers?

If humanity wants children
we must raise them
in the flesh and the spirit of women,
in the flesh and the spirit of men.

We must all become mothers
to each other
before the womb of the world
will kindle any future.

—Anitra L. Freeman

MOTHER ESCAPES

Fourteen years ago my mother was
locked in a little room at St. Francis Cabrini
Hospital, because we didn't know what else to do
back then.

But Mother knew.

Mother knew lots better things to do
than to be locked up in a little room
in Spring.

She used her teeth
to rip her down pillow open.
With handfuls of soft white feathers
she blew clouds under the door
and yelled "Fire! ... Fire!"

An orderly actually came.
He really threw open the door.

Faster than a naked toddler
Mother skinned under his arm
zipped down the hall
slammed through the main doors
and ran down the sidewalk.

three-o-clock in the afternoon broad daylight
92 pounds in a flapping hospital gown
long wiry black hair
and feathers.
Yelling "Fire!"

Mother told me the story herself.
I was never so proud of her.
To this day
I stand a little straighter
when I have feathers in my hair.

—*Anitra L. Freeman*

MY FATHER'S ARMS

My mother held me like a desperately
long-awaited answer.
My father held me like a question
that I could never hear.
My grandfather held me like a flag.

When I embrace my friends
I listen with my skin
and with my breath,
let love soak slowly from my pores
and stay until they drop their grip
and stand up straight.

Sometimes I just lie on the grass
and breathe.
The sky watches my face
until I sleep.

If I imagine how
I'd like to feel the arms of God,
I would like the Father to hold me
like someone who was looking at my face,
like someone who was safe to fall asleep on,
like someone who knew how.

—Anitra L. Freeman

MY GRANDFATHER'S EYE

My grandfather had one eye.
Everyone was fascinated —
Kids could show it.
He usually wore a glass eye in the socket,
but he could pop it out and pass it around
just like a marble.
Sometimes he wore a black patch like a pirate.
Sometimes he just let the barren lid
lie there and pulse.

He told us a different story every day
about how he lost his eye.
He'd grown up on a farm —
he told us once a mule had kicked the back of his head so hard
his eyeball flew right out over the cornfield.
The next day a pitchfork had poked it out
during haying season — that's why
you don't get careless handling pitchforks and such.
He'd been a lumberjack — a falling tree
had scratched his eye out;
a flying ember from the cookfire
fried his eyeball in the socket
just like an egg in a pan.
He used to smoke, and we shouldn't ever —
he smoked a cigar down too close once
and burned his own eye out.
I spent an entire evening
silent, puzzling about that one —
I think that's why he told it to me.

When I was sixteen he told me
his Dad used to beat him when he drank.
He used to beat him with a chain.

—*Anitra L. Freeman*

RESURRECTION

A poem for Easter Sunday 4/11/04
Dedicated to Liz Smith
who always rises

He proved it once.
The spirit always rises.
From fear and hatred,
Power and war,
Greed and envy,
All denial —
The spirit always rises.

From history's birth
On crude clay tablets
To its end
In some far star —
The spirit always rises.
From ignorance and terror,
From narrowness and pain.
From starvation and rejection —
The spirit always rises.

Give all your strength to what you hope for;
Do not bend your knee to death.
Do not bend your heart to power.
Do not bend your mind to pain.
Evil never lasts forever.

The spirit always rises.

—Anitra L. Freeman

ROBERTO MAESTAS LANE

*Dedicated to Roberto Maestas, the Executive Director
of El Centro de la Raza, the host of Tent Village 3 homeless
encampment from July 16, 2000 to January 16, 2001.*

At El Centro de la Raza
a stretched line of tarpaulins
carries a hand-lettered sign
"Roberto Maestas Lane."

At one end three men sit in folding chairs
elbows on knees,
watching a portable television.
At the other end a man lays on a cot
chin on palm
reading a book.

In the rotunda above
there is food;
a picnic of survival.
At the other end of the camp
security watch digs out blankets
for newcomers.

Along the roads friends come
bringing food and clothing.
Along the roads
people go back and forth to work.

We make roads for each other
into the future.
We carry each other's lives.

—*Anitra L. Freeman*

SHARING CITY SHELTER

Warmth, convenience, shelter from the elements.
Bus shelters.

Of course, if they are too closed in they become unsafe
anything can happen in there
so we'll have an open front
glass sides
with big gaps
and a tiny little roof
and it's still a shelter
you can't possibly get more than half-drowned in there.

It is still an attraction to those homeless people

so we'll take out the benches
it is harder to drown when you're standing up

and now everyone, shoppers and commuters and the poor
can huddle together on equally sore feet in the driving rain
in our community bus shelters.

—*Anitra L. Freeman*

SURVIVAL PROGRAM

How do we mourn a hundred children?
    Feel the absence of one small hand
    and then another.
How do we mourn a hundred women?
    Name one silent voice
    and then one other.
How do we mourn a hundred
fathers, brothers, lovers?
    Trace the shape of one missing face
    and then one more.
How do we save a thousand lives?
    Hold one hand
    Listen to one voice
    Look in one face
    at a time.

—*Anitra L. Freeman*

SURVIVORS

Damn the child that screams and bites
Answers late kindness with bitter anger

Damn all prey turned predator
Children claiming streets and alleys
Tiny faces with feral eyes

Damn the women who prowl
With stolen jaguar claws
Who refuse to come inside
Again

Save our pity for the
     sweet
     innocent
     dead

—Anitra L. Freeman

THE MAP IS NOT THE TERRITORY

Eskimos have a hundred words for snow.
Here in the land that made dysfunctional famous
we have one word for one thousand realities:
depression.

open your eyes to the faded ceiling
stare without interest
fall asleep again

rock on the toilet
stare at the razor on the sink
teetering on the edge

walk through a crowd
stare ahead fixedly
ignore all the saw-edged
whispers of your name

   walk through a crowd
   hearing nothing

my bones have turned to concrete
my flesh bruises itself on them

   I do not touch
   I do not taste
   my body is a feather
   anchored in nothing

I will never stop weeping

   I will never cry again

rock and bone have turned villain

   I am all that is wrong with Life

Daddy came in at midnight
it has been midnight ever since

   I lost my Daddy to cancer
   I am lost

everything is fine
and I don't give a damn

I need more than a hundred words.

—*Anitra L. Freeman*

UNTITLED

In my heart,
armored against all invasion,
one lone arrow.

—Anitra L.Freeman

WHAT IS FAMILY?

Family are the shouts in the dark that keep you awake
      trying to be invisible under your blankets.
Family is the warm heart you run to
      when everyone else at the rink skates too fast
      and you've cut your knees on the ice.
Family are given to you at birth
      with your eyes and lips and nose.
They will stick to you wherever you go
      and shape how you see
      and what you say
      and how you are seen
      forever.
Family are found new each day
      wherever you put your heart last.
Family are the people you share bread with,
      and whoever you share the lack of bread with.
Sometimes your family aren't people.
Family is whoever lives under the tent of your soul.
Your family can be as big as you are,
      and from birth to death, your real, real family
      are the ones who make you grow bigger.

—*Anitra L. Freeman*

WHY HOPE?

Jello died at twenty-seven,
homeless, Independence Day in the City of Angels,
died of the damage of escaping one more time.
Too Short died on Greyhound,
coming back from her man in the City of Angels,
died of the damage from reconciling one more time.
Chrissy died in hospital,
here in Seattle,
died of the cancer, one too many years out on the street.

Why do I hope?
Because Barbie's attempted suicide failed,
and she called me.
Because Melissa comes in to write about her anger,
instead of hiding in it.
Because Sean is working,
and Kevin has a place to stay.

I came to the wrong planet to find perfection.

I came to the right planet to find work.

—*Anitra L. Freeman*

"WORDS"

Your pain is not important.
You can't complain
because Mother's hands traced hourglasses
and she thrust her hips out
and made smacking noises
over your full breasted figure
when you were thirteen
and Daddy hid his magazines
but told you the jokes anyway
while his eyes traced your full breasted figure
when you were thirteen
and Mom dragged you out of bed
and took you to a neighbor's house
because Daddy was out drinking
and she expected anything of him
he was a bastard
he might kill her
he might rape you
when you were thirteen.
It was only words.

You can't complain.
Others were raped
beaten
bloody
by fathers, mothers, strangers,
cops.
You were only assaulted
with words.

You've been called crazy,
divorced, fired,
your son won't talk to his crazy Mom,
lots of friends won't talk to you again,
but you can't complain.

You haven't been locked up, tied down, burned through
with electricity,
shot up with so much thorazine
you bled from every opening from your ears
to your cunt.

You've been lost and cold and hungry
but never for long enough.
You've never been trespassed out of the welfare office,
arrested out of the hospital,
shot for stealing a loaf of bread;
you
can't complain.

You have to heal the world
because everybody else's pain
is more important than yours
is more real than yours
yours is only words.

But
dig underneath the words
and you will find
a heart knotted like a trumpet.
You can sound that heart
in words
and the other wounded hearts
echo.

These words are blood,
chips of white bone.
These words have stripped the flesh from your back,
and they can rebuild it.

It is never
only words.

—*Anitra Freeman*

YOUR MANY KINDNESSES

"In an unjust system kindness is not enough."
—the father of Sister Helen Prejean

to be kind
the counselor told me
there was nothing wrong with me
I was not at all like my mother
sent me home with exercises to relax me
to talk me through the times my mind burned up the world
the times the world opened to drop me into a void

to be kind
the staff of shelters
served food and brought pillows and poured coffee
and piled helplessness upon helplessness
and smiled as women smile for empty bodies

to be kind
the neighbors want the new shelter
to be someplace more appropriate
someplace where there are already
more people of that kind

to be kind
the businessmen would like to study
the need and design and the placement
of hygiene centers in the business core
a little longer, long enough, perhaps,
that all the unpleasant people will go away

to be kind
we will no longer sell
forty-ounce bottles of beer
in the districts where the worn men sleep
because it is not good for them

their drunken ravings frighten us
and maybe, maybe they will go away

to be kind
we will look away from our friend when she cries
to be kind
we will look away from the fear in the small gray woman
at the desk next door
we will look away from her disappearance
to be kind
we will look away from the child screaming at his father
we will look away from the smack of flesh on bone
to be kind
I will not tell you
what your kindness means to me

—*Anitra L. Freeman*

WHY I HAVE NOT COMMITTED SUICIDE

The Devil sat me down to lunch
in a little crimson room.
He fed me on tea brewed from fresh hot tears
and cakes baked of violet gloom.

The tea was bitter and the cakes were hard
and I sweated from every pore,
but better such bitter fare, I said,
than the cold outside that door.

Yes, better the Devil's crimson room
and the Devil's crimson laughter
than the awful cold outside that door,
and silence, forever after.

—Peg Howard, 1965

This is the only poem of my mother's I still have. She died in 1982. In 1978, she had finally been diagnosed as manic-depressive, stabilized on Lithium, and began attending AA — no longer needing to self-medicate on alcohol. She assisted her psychiatrist in helping women make the transition from hospitalization back to independent living. I knew her best in those last few years. It has been in these last few years, since being diagnosed manic-depressive myself, and treated, that I have really learned to appreciate her strength.

Mom — I do still love you.

—Anitra L. Freeman

LEGEND

Thoughts take shape and wing,
telling stories out of time,
in a place where there was still mystery and wonder,
told by women sitting close to Byzantine fire.
Their children clutch at skirts
mother scented
and remember.
Each generation taking on a new facet,
each story woven into a tapestry of miracles.
There is blue smoke weaving around us,
telling and close
of those times
when there was still myth and innocence
in Byzantine fire.

—*Catherine Gainey*

MOON

If,
in a moment frantic
my mad beauty,
I
tiny moan
could see you then,
when it felt
honeyful
live, ache, drunk
still after love.
My delirious goddess
we
worship a moon
lake rain and blue;
The summer gift.
A woman some enormous
power
less part delicate sleep.

—*Catherine Gainey*

MY HANDS HAVE CHANGED

My hands have changed.
They are not the expressions of me that once were ornamental.
No longer lovely reflections of my daily habit:
a manifestation perhaps of something else.

These hands were happy to create imperfect water-
color landscapes
on the backs of paper bags, a little girl dipping
brushes into Daddy's coffee cup.

These once dimpled fingers
navigated the mystery of my mother's hair.
My little hands were swallowed up by Daddy's
much larger, callused ones,
grimacing at the feel.

I have spent many fueled hours in
contemplation of shapely nails, mended with Crazy Glue,
carefully mended. "A lady's hands reveal her habits,"
my mother's eternal lecture drumming incessantly.
For me they made perfect camouflage.

Now my hands are quite unlovely,
years of ammonia and bleach took their toll.
My hands have changed,
they have built a home,
they can tear all manner of vegetable.

They are strong now—no longer lovely, yet
beautiful beyond words.
Older than they should be, perhaps, wrinkled from worry,
but they are mine.
I often marvel at their wisdom.
My hands tell a story,
a roadmap of my life, beginning to end,
as it should be.
They carry more than they should,
however capable.

—*Catherine Gainey*

EYES OF REALITY

When you talk to people
at an angle
instead of on a level plane
you're trying to avoid looking
into the eyes of reality

—*Sylvia G.*

BUS STOP, 7:45 A.M.

November storm
leaves blowing down
thicker than the rain

—*Glinda*

WHAT IS FREEDOM?

The ability to feel safe in your own home.
The ability to feel safe in your own country.
Protected from harm
      - from robbers and from drunkards
      - from terrorists and from bombs
With a few bucks in your pocket
      - for food
      - for a book
      - for a haircut
With enough in the bank to
      - pay the rent
      - pay for the phone
      - pay the bills
With enough spare time to
      - go to a concert
      - go to a movie
      - enjoy a workshop
With enough joy to
      - share with others who have less
      - share yourself with another
      - spread joy unselfconsciously
With enough love of God to
      - share in church on Sunday
      - share by giving unstintingly
      - share by praying unceasingly

—Susi Henderson

CHOCO-LUNE

Chocolates and truffles.
Sweetness applied to my palate
Good. Better. Best.

—Susi Henderson

IN MYSELF I KEEP A SECRET

In myself I keep a secret.
it tells me all I need to know
about why you live in constant crisis,
and why your urgent pleas sound so much like anger
when you ask for help from those of us who listen.
You don't know we've been there too.

There are lots of us with secrets
who know the feelings and the score.
And why your children cry more often,
and they keep their eyes down more
than all the other children
'cause they're threatened, 'cause they're scared
and they're hungry for a future
they aren't sure is there.

In myself I keep a secret,
in my heart I know your pain
and how your fear becomes the normal
and you wonder if you're sane.
Maybe we don't really see you;
we couldn't really know or care
how close you are to wanting off the planet.

I've been there ...

—Kathryn Henne

TAKE BACK THE NIGHT

A crowd of a thousand women
demanding justice and reform
were gathered, and heard by many
who had been also raped and torn
but who were too meek to walk with us
who were too mild to speak up
against their own attackers who stood with them
while we marched.

What were those women thinking
while their husbands smirked and jeered?
Were they thinking we looked angry,
unfeminine or weird?
Did they think it was acceptable
to let us march alone
as if we'll win the battle
without every woman's vote?
But we'll march and shout and rally
even if you are not there;
for us to stand by silent is to say we do not care.
No more women shall die from violence.
No more children shall live in fear
of the fathers and the uncles.
We (the women) will make it safer here.

—Kathryn Henne

SISTER

Sister I need to talk
I've passed through a mental block
you're on shore and I'm at sea
alone in Santiago Chile
explaining my fears to flowers
        in tears
wishing you were here to protect me
because the flowers are the fears
which bring me tears
because they're all I have ever wanted to be.

—Beth H.

FULL MOON

Underground shelters one year
How high the moon?
is it still china-white against
a velvet midnight
the smell of fresh water
the look between lovers

sterling light silent across a ripe vineyard
cooled fruit full of damp harvest moon?

—*Catherine Hunt*

UNTITLED

Trying to get close to my mother was like
getting close with a vacuum sweeper.
And being close with my father
has been being close with a lawn mower.

My family ends here.

I begin here.

—Catherine Hunt

MANY IS THE TIME

Many is the time I stood at another vigil — not knowing which way to turn.

Many is the time I cried — until I felt like I had died.

Many is the time I wanted to smash my head into the wall — because Mayor Greg Nickels wouldn't take a call ...

Many is the time I felt like hating Ron Sims because he was too busy running for Governor of Washington to give Women In Black a phone call.

Then I thought I heard God say:

I have heard the cries of Women In Black, I have seen you at each vigil.

Weep no more, my ladies, for someday, who will stand for these politicians who didn't give a second thought to not returning your call. For as sure as the sun comes up tomorrow, they will see great sorrow.

Go now, you Women In Black, let Me carry the load.

For as I have seen you today I surely won't turn these homeless people away.

For every tear you cried, I caught them before they dried.

Put these people in my hands and together we will stand.

—*Mona Joyner*

WEARY

weary,
I walk
searching
for my voice
my dignity
my respect

in desperation
I speak out
reach out
volunteer
only to be
ignored
ridiculed
disrespected
in return

my degree
means nothing
my good intentions
even less

yet I hold on
to the hope
my God-given talents
will mean something
somewhere

—*Kitty K.*

DICKENSIAN

I grew up as a lonely child.
The stars, blank and groaning things.
The birds, selfish, thin and bleak.
My dreams filled with chimney sweeps.
I could not see past dark and cold.
I did not know a loving touch.
I did not know a kindly word.
I made my way without these things.
I grew up fierce, forgiving none.
I learned to have a shifty tongue.
I never sang, I never cried.
I found the places shadows fell.
I made myself a home inside.
Alone, I watched the moon grow fat
Then disappear and saw the truth
Of how I'd leave the earth one day,
In silence, save for rustling trees.

—Mercedes Lawry

EXACT CHANGE

for services rendered, we offer coin
or the imagined idea of currency,
symbolic flame of wealth or labor,
accumulated trust like a fence to keep
the dismal at bay while the same woman
stands at the freeway entrance,
day after day, like a mannequin holding
the cardboard sign that sums her life:
3 children, need food. A practical
vacancy in her eyes, is she real,
we wonder, passing with our window up,
is she honest or a con, part of a clever
conspiracy to make a living,
not so different from most.
She stands in the rain, in bright
March sun while daffodils begin to open
all over the city. The furious need for money
takes precedence. We trade our minds and hearts,
our time and finally, our hopes
for the warm bed, whatever it takes
to keep our place on the spinning globe.

—*Mercedes Lawry*

PLUS OR MINUS TEETH

And at night I sing my heart out for the world (by force and due to threats on my person).

They all just love my old voice.

There's just a few difficulties about it all.

All the earnings are squashed.

Due to all of force injuring and threatening me in transit.

And the world will identify me for all of my earnings.

There are just a few problems about that.

Will my teeth (what few are left) still be there in the morning?
Will I still be walking from "Boots the Cat" planting his foot on my ruptured and fractured spine?

JESUS WAS BEAT TO A PULP, BEFORE HE FINALLY WAS HUNG ON
A CROSS TO DIE FOR ALL MANKIND.

In this world, there aren't thank yous for the holy.

—*Carol A. Leno*

HOW DO I PUT INTO WORDS…

How do I put into words
        the feelings
that are still there
        of a trauma long ago
My chest hurts from the anxiety
        My stomach aches
from the knot the size of a man's fist
        punching me and knocking
the wind out of me
        The nightmares start again
and continue to go round and round
        so tired restless can't sleep
the feelings of terror and helplessness
        of feeling insane
and out of control
        Who's knocking at the gates
to let Pandora out of her box
        to torment and tear me apart
This thing that has been
        a part of my life
for so many years
        Just won't go away
It's always under the surface
        waiting to expose itself
again and again
        Burying me in pain and hurt
Will I ever have peace
        Perhaps not until I pass
to the other side.

—*Madeline Lewis*

ONLY ELEVEN

Now I have a new baby brother
I have to help
take care of him too
along with my little sister
When can I play I'm only eleven

Now you tell me my Grandfather
is coming to live with us
I have to help look after him
because he's old
When can I play I'm only twelve

My mother is becoming ill
I have to look after her
When can I play I'm only thirteen

The house needs to be cleaned
and meals cooked
school work has to be done
When can I play I'm only fourteen

Taking care of so many family members
doing so much stuff
When can I play I'm only fifteen

The years have slipped by
marriages, children, work,
taking care of so many
When can I play I'm only fifty

Now I can play
but is it safe or OK
I don't know how to play
I'm only fifty-two

—*Madeline Lewis*

SECRET KEEPER

I am the keeper of secrets
to the world on the outer
I shine and smile brightly
My appearance does not
indicate anything other than
all is right with the world.

But inside there is buried
anger I haven't reached yet
Sometimes the pain is so
intense I can't breathe

Which man is standing on
my chest this time, grandfather,
father, husband, boss, who else

I thought I left the abuse
behind. Instead it's buried
inside—like Pandora's box—
once the lid has been
removed all manner
of demons arise.

—*Madeline Lewis*

TOUCHING

You touched me,
I asked you not to
but you did it anyway.

You caused me
pain and shame
but you did it anyway.

You said this won't hurt
but you could not feel the pain
and you did it anyway.

You had been drinking,
and I said "don't touch me."
but you did it anyway.

You took my power away.
I asked you not to but
you did it anyway.

Give me back my power
I asked you to.

I said, "you won't touch me again."
I have my power back
You didn't do it anymore.

—*Madeline Lewis*

MILLENNIAL FAREWELL

Steam rising from rooftops
I savor my first cup
Sun peeks in
Through even
Death-bleak December

—*Kathleen Mitchell*

T.P.

Woman, 40ish
Mounts Metro
Pays with a pass
Clutches a 12-pack of
Toilet paper
Unbaggable
And instantly I know

Hour's round trip to
Some super, 'cause
When you're down to
Your last five dollars
You darn well gotta
Take advantage
Of a sale that good.

—Kathleen Mitchell

WAR BABY 2000

I'm not the only one
That loved too hard
And hoped too long
Worked wrinkles
Gray streaks into my
"If I had a bell"

But the song I've sung
Through a daisy chain
Of diaper pins and
Grocery bags
By God! I sing it
Louder than hell

—*Kathleen Mitchell*

BEING AN ALIVE WOMAN

I am an
Alive Woman,
Determined to live a long, long time,
Getting older and bolder with each new day,
Knowing deep within
The longer I am around the stronger
I will become.
And I do not intend to wait around
to be free.

I am an Alive Woman, Alive woman,
Red ruby womb,
All my own, all my own,
With each full moon my powers become
Stronger, freer, wilder, wiser.

I am an Alive Woman
alive to my strength
Alive to my power,
Alive to the cycles of being a woman,

Determined to have my voice heard,
I have emerged body, mind, and spirit,
Loving
All of who I am
Being
All of who I am

—*Marcia Moonstar*

FREEDOM TIME

It is time to be free,
time to get real,
Stand tall, stand proud, stand together,
Stay together even if it's rainy or sunny weather,

It is time to get in touch with reality,
Time to break the chains of poverty, addictions, and afflictions
be strong, have courage, stand tall, stand proud,
stand together, day or night,

It's time to believe we have the right
To have some heaven here on earth
Believe there is a better tomorrow,

It is time to let go of our sorrow,
Our date with fate
And give faith a chance,
Look to a brighter day,
Where we will not tolerate discrimination of any kind,

It is time to protect your rights,
time to fight for our rights,
Even in the darkest of times.

We all need to open our hearts from the beginning,
Spread hope, understanding and love from the heaven above
In the light of day and the dark of night,

It is time to free your soul and stay in control,
Time to free your mind and be kind,
Time to free your spirit and be truly alive,
Feeling spring in the air, and summer in your heart,
Everyday is freedom day, Everyday is freedom day.

—*Marcia Moonstar*

DÉJA VU

Lately I've been experiencing
déjà vu
feels like a time and place
that has happened before
unfinished business
I watch and remember what I see
events that have happened over
sixty years ago resurfacing to
be attended to.
I feel the outcome will be
different the spirit of the people
and the Earth has changed.
I watch and I wonder what I
will do, am
I doing my part?

—*Ruanda Morrison*

DISAPPEARING ACT

I know you, know me.
We used to run in the same circle
of acquaintances.
Sharing opinions, ideas,
seeing each other at public events.
I always considered you a friend.
I lost my job.
The work I found paid so much less.
To compensate I worked two, then three jobs.
I lost time to socialize and attend social events.
This I'm sure is when I began to disappear.
I was injured in an accident.
I could not work.
I became a burden to my partner.
My partner and I split up.
We are now friends, only that,
I'm too proud to go for friendship or advice.
I lost my home.
Over time I've lost most of my possessions.
I live in transitional housing and shelters.
I'm unemployed, no income all outgo.
I tell myself that material things can be replaced.
Material friends can always he found.
I have my spirit, healthy body, and mind.
I still see you on the street sometimes.
I remember when we used to speak.
You don't seem to remember me, nor do you speak
I've become a stranger to you.
The disappearing act is complete.

—*Ruanda Morrison*

I AM WOMAN

There is more to perceive than the curves of me.
I speak with confidence and respect.
I expect to give and receive basic respect,
and earn the rest.
I know you can't give nor
receive something you've never had.
I'm a thinker of thoughts, shallow and deep.
I can do what ever I set my mind to.
I'm aware of power and I use it in the best way possible
working not to abuse it or be abused by others wielding power,

I'm looking for a power exchange not a giveaway.
Freedom is expensive, well worth its cost. I will pay.
Free is not always good. Knowledge is power.
There is no excuse for ignorance.
Integrity, honesty, may seem invisible like the wind, more than words
these ideas can be acted on and results felt.
These are actions I do in my daily life that mean a lot to me.
I am a woman, one of many, legion. When I was made there was no
mold to break. I'm one of a kind completely original.
I AM A WOMAN

—*Ruanda Morrison*

OUR SELVES ALONE

From looking at my past, you can't get a view;
thru the window that comes up in front of you ...
to hear my story, you wouldn't have a clue,
that one could have a past so blue ...

Life can be a vicious circle that no one understands,
the only one to break is in the one that can withstand ...
Life can be a vicious circle and you're the only one that
can truly take command ...

Anyone can want for you and everyone can care
but; no one can direct you, cause you're the only
one that's there ...

—*Wendy Nakashima*

WITHOUT BLUES

*For all those who have seen drugs, alcoholism
and abuse tear their families apart.*

Without the stub of crocus,
the breeze through cedar
and hills to climb
in the soft light of January
I would be lost.

Without the picket lines'
"How you doing?"—
friends sitting around at the table
while November rains,
I would wash away in tears.

Without my pencil,
the work that must be done,
the brothers and sisters
in the strong August sun,
I would go over the edge.

—Lonnie Nelson

ODE TO BOB SANTOS

Here's a gentlemen,
    Who does a lot,
For everyone around him,
    He helps us all of us.

We call him our Uncle Bob,
    He's our favorite uncle,
He calls us his favorite nieces,
    To help us keep a roof over our heads.

To keep us free from harm,
    while we stay safe and warm,
He's provided us a dry place,
    To rest our weary heads at night.

—Vivian Nelson

SELF-PROTECTION

There are times in life
        That after a while
We should just try to forget,
        leave them in our personal file.

They are part of our personal history.
        We shouldn't wear them
On our shirtsleeves
        For everyone to see them.

Learn to walk around
        With an air of safety
While we learn to defend ourselves.
        Some may learn karate.

There must be other
        means of self-defense
That will help us and that
        Will all make sense.

—*Vivian Nelson*

SELF-PORTRAIT
May 13, 1960 — August 3, 2005

Cynthia Lee Ozimek was born the daughter of an opera singer and sculptor turned steel worker on May 13, 1960. Raised in Pittsburgh, Pennsylvania, she attended college at St. Petersburg Junior College in Tarpon Springs, Florida and lived in both the states of Georgia and Arizona before moving to Seattle in the early 1990s.

Despite suffering the ramifications of homelessness in the literal sense, Cynthia has found great joy, solace and belonging in the community of women where she has resided, on and off, for the past several years.

To this end, she has made it her mission, through the written and spoken word, to advocate on behalf of those individuals in Seattle's homeless women's community who, for whatever reason, have found themselves on the outskirts of the society in which they reside. Cynthia believes that each one of God's children has, within themselves, the power to positively affect the world in any number of ways. Her biggest dream is to publish a book of essays, vignettes and stories on the women with whom she communes each day.

In addition to being a contributing writer for *Real Change*, Seattle's newspaper for the poor and homeless, Ms. Ozimek is also a member of the *Real Change* Homeless Speaker's Bureau, a group of homeless and formerly homeless individuals who strive through public speaking to educate their community on both the facts and fallacies related to both the cause and the consequences of homelessness.

While she looks forward to soon having a home of her own, Cynthia believes that home is truly where the heart is. Thus, her lack of physical shelter is not as important as one might think; Cynthia is blessed to have a multitude of "homes" in the eyes, the lives and the hearts of the women she lives with, writes and speaks about.

—*Cynthia Ozimek*

FALLEN ANGELS

Sad
I have again
found my rhythm
behind these crumbling walls
that stretch so high above my life
within the games of spades and the plastic cups of coffee and the sisters who
cradle the
streets as easily as they welcome me.

In
this day
at this moment
I am no different than any other
my beginnings and endings blended into red felon's cloth
and the metallic glimmer of handcuffs ... but at night, this night
I dream of God's strength and I read the words embedded into these walls
by those whose deaths were foretold by the judges and the jailers and the
system that
barely knew them.

I
have knelt
in the silence of the indifferent
no one believing that anything of value was left inside of me.
I have been gutted and laid open like a fish by those whose eyes have
refused to meet my
own because in all of the days and months and years of my life's desecration
I had fallen so
far and so fast and so hard it was believed I could not survive and, thus,
deemed worthless, it
was thought best simply to cut the loss of me and to turn away.

I
don't
deny my past
but neither have I perished.
I may scream. I may be silent.
I may simply set my sight upon the furthest star above the darkest sea but as
I swim I will
gather my dreams and upon them I will build an island.

I
am imperfect
and I am alone
and in the sands of sleepless nights and winter dreams,
outside of this mortar, beyond the alleys of my despair I walk with eyes held
high. I am
poised to find those, who like me were given up for dead or declared missing
in action.

They
too have
unfinished dreams
amid the shadows of fallen angels
lost long before these walls made before me.

—*Cynthia L. Ozimek*

FOR TODAY

I am thankful
To be amongst the only people with whom I have ever fitted in.
I am not talking about preachers, police or physics teachers ...
I am referring to women
Who are refugees of violence ...
I am talking about mothers who have been abandoned by their children ...
I am talking about children abandoned to drugs ...
I am talking about schizophrenic poets and disaffected dreamers and artists who paint
between
the lines of azure skies and fifths of rye.

I
Am
Talking about
Lying with a fever on a broken couch,
feeling as if you were a part of no one
And having a total stranger approach with a cup of tea and a stolen blanket
And covering you with a kindness you seldom offer yourself.

I
Am
Talking about
Holding a stranger as she cries,
not walking past a ragged hand.
I am talking about buying a cigarette for someone when you do not smoke,
Or giving your coat and your last five dollars to a runaway who looks into your eyes
And swears she's eighteen, with someplace to go, some one to meet, somewhere to live
Other than the streets ...
I am talking about caring when no one else does, when there's nothing much to gain.
When caring breaks all the rules
It is usually caring at its best.

Today
I am thankful
That for a moment I am free of the cold and rain
That falls with abandon upon the city, upon the homeless, upon my soul.

Let
The winter come;
We will fire the snow with kindness.

Let the darkness fall; we will ferry the way with wind-blown candles.
Let the lightning strike; we will capture its light for fallen dreams.

Let
No one,
No one be forgotten
Because she is old, or without a dollar, or absent family or friends.

I
Am
Talking
About God
And the power of love
And the comfort of strangers.
When your world seems like it's falling apart, it is the odd leap of faith,
the one who risks her heart, who break the rules, who reaches out.
In the contest of life, it is the one who gives
who truly, truly wins

—*Cynthia L. Ozimek*

ONLY HUMAN

Parkinsons
is, for me, a recurrent affliction.
It strikes me when I am standing in front of microphones
or saying, "I love you," or wearing a pair of those black knee
length polyester shorts
that remind me of something my mother might have worn ...

Where adulthood
encroaches upon the child
I have rediscovered my lack of grace
and cringe upon those steps which send me flying across the
sidewalk
or careening into trees and, once, in the
shower I caught myself singing, "Feelings,"
by Barry Manilow
and I really felt sick because it is such a
nauseating song.

Where
adulthood
encroaches upon the child
I have discovered that life is a parody of
errors
and that I am destined to repeat everyone of
them.

And
despite the fact
that I have the guilty conscience
and the arthritic knees of all good Catholics
everywhere
somewhere my mother is rolling over in her
grave because my lover is a woman
and because I routinely show up at hospital
emergency rooms
without wearing underwear.

Thus
should I suffer
a nervous breakdown
while standing in front of you here
tonight
please ... please ... please remember
that providence is my preferred
provider
and that I fed stray cats and that I
was, after all
only human.

—*Cynthia Ozimek*

SLEEPLESS IN SEATTLE / THE MANIC SHUFFLE

Morning shadows
Skirt dawn's irascible walls
As I pray to Saint Serta Sealy Posturpedic, the angel of sleep deprivation
For the privilege of packing it in.

What
Do you do
When the tea and honey's spent, the books have all been read
And you've turned off your television in abject horror
Because you've actually found yourself sympathizing with a balding, 60-year old wanna be
vampire appearing at three am on the "Jenny Jones" show.

What
Do you do
When your mind just won't shut down
And even the dog is hip to your karma and refuses to sleep with you
Because all of your ups and downs disturb his dreams.

Most
Often, I am a likeable person
But at bedtime I have come to abhor every lover I have ever known.
"I AM TALKING LIFE AND DEATH HERE," I have implored
to increasingly rhythmic snores.

Years spent
Watching lovers sleep
And animals move to different rooms.

It
Is an exhausting profession
Keeping watch o'er the world
But as I wearily pad by the snoring partner and the dream swept dog
To drain yet another gallon of chamomile tea I can't help but to think with a scant
Measure of satisfaction: If the sky does fall one night, some time,
I will be the first to know.

—*Cynthia Ozimek*

THE PIANO

For each note
the piano sends blithely into turbulent air
melodic sound follows, rifts across the sky,
leave no choice but to follow.

Tonight music plays
but stars lie wearily in eyes
there is no comfort in sound, in ivory keys,
reaper of poetry & death,
music which has ceased but never within me.

I have
wanted to die since I was nine.
I watched her piano destroyed, pieces of
mahogany & death strewn across childhood's roof
like so much garbage…
I have wanted to die since I was nine, feeling like
the piano, unceremoniously dragged across the
roof of my home & dumped into an empty lot…
I have wanted to die since I was nine because
without music,
without my mother, I felt like no one.

At night, bitter chords strike,
attempting to re-create the music, the bridge they
once walked upon.

Winter then,
breaking limbs when the last note fell.
Music soothes the broken limbs, speaks to winds
which have stolen my voice.
and my Mother's piano, the sweetest, sweetest of
all sounds.

—*Cynthia Lee Ozimek*

THE SMOKING ROOM

Many
Heads lay
Upon these broken tables.
It is 7 a.m. and time is still. Still moving, still weeping,
Still weary, still seeping,
Still breathing like a cancerous lung
Rasping in my ear,
Sad and beautiful, intricate and bare, desolate and free.
Cold as a heater blows and mixes with ashes.
Scattered about the room
Smoke and madness.

—Cynthia Lee Ozimek

MY LIFE SEEMS TO BE MADE UP OF WAITING NOW:

My life seems to be made up of waiting now:

Waiting for housing,
Waiting for the end of a "Hot Flash",
Waiting for the laundry,
Waiting for a shower,
Waiting to lie down,
Waiting for a prescription to be filled,
Waiting for a meal,

Before I used to make things happen,
Now I wait for them.

—*Peaches*

SITTING IN THE CORNER, AT THE MALL…

Sitting in the corner, at the Mall, shopping bags at
my feet, trying to blend in.

Washing in the sink, at the Greyhound station,
checking my watch every few minutes, like I am
waiting for a bus.

I've started chewing my nails again, a habit I had
given up in the 10th grade. Nerves worn to a frazzle,
I wait for a letter from home.

—*Peaches*

RECIPE FOR HOMELESSNESS

3 cups of "Sorry, we're not hiring."
2 cups of unpaid bills.
1 cup of "Pay the rent or else."
½ dozen "I'm sorry's."
½ tsp of "I don't cares."

Combine all ingredients in a heated discussion of "you-should-haves" in an ostracizer or conventional blender. Bake in a preheated oven of hopelessness for too long. Keep chilled and fresh with feelings of helplessness and top with a liberal dab of being called "FAILURE."

yield: Homeless.
Persons served: UNLIMITED, any age.

—Mary Phillips

PEOPLE

People say I am fat.
I say they are not skinny.

People say I am ugly.
I say they are not pretty.

People like starting fights with me.
I try to stand my ground
and I get into trouble.

People say I am afraid to fight.
Do you want to know something?

They are right!

—Robin P.

HOMEBODY'S SONG

I yearn to sleep in peace and absolute dead quiet
To sleep in
To not have to go out at all
To take a long long bubble bath, uninterrupted of course
To not have to wear clothes all day if not all week
To masturbate
To watch TV or VCR movies
To listen to music at my own volume without the benefit of headphones
To be with my darling precious cuddly cat
Queen Sheba Elizabeth Her Royal Highness
To eat food, but not right away
To drink ice water or eat ice cream
To sew, to crochet, to knit
To read, to write in my own time
Not by the white man's time or the shelter's time
My time
Someday soon
Very, very soon
My time could not come fast enough
However when it does
Good morning
Welcome home
It's been a song long long long time coming.

—Radha

UNTITLED

it's sunday and angeline's women's day shelter is closed because there wasn't enough staff, and the library is closed because there wasn't enough funding, and the security guard at the food court told me the bathroom's closed to non-customers, and i reeeeeeaaaaaaally gotta go.

i finally got my laundry done. i have a job interview in a few hours ... where can i keep this bag until *after* the interview?

i didn't KNOW!!! well, i did know that angeline's would only store my laundry until they closed at 6, and i thought i'd be back by then, but they liked me and had someone else interview me, and i didn't want to use their phone so that they could hear me ask angeline's to please hold my laundry ... so i think i might have the job, and no clothes to wear to it.

i got the job and a regular bed in a shelter. the lady next to me snores louder than a chainsaw in an echo chamber, and i haven't gotten any sleep this week. i shake her, staff wakes her, and she turns over and begins again.

i had a one-bedroom apartment. now i have a 4' square locker. where do i put my couch? hell, where do i put my *shoes*?

funny thing is, i always pictured camping as a relatively easy lifestyle. except, i have nowhere to put my pack except on my back. when i had a home, i could leave things there.

recipe for seattle bean soup: put beans in a pot. when rain stops, light fire.

—*Rango*

UNTITLED

sing a song of violation
equivocation
demarcation
supplication
tribulation
and truncation

sing a song of subterfuge
a deadly ruse
loving abuse
and splitting in twos
and no way to choose

sing a song of fighting free
a warrior's creed
survival fees
pstd
and healing mes

—Rango

MS. ANN IS DEAD

I thought she loved me
I wanted friends to be

Old, frightened and locked down
we left hell for the same town

First day free, a smile & cash
my money stopped, her love didn't last

"I'll show you," I pouted
all my kindness rerouted

She worked me from greed
I wanted to share what she'd need

She seemed of late ...
better going than coming

At 11 am I was her claim to fame
at midnight, she was not the same

up against a wall looking for something ...

Those people didn't have it
but, they kept her pipe lit

12:30 should I say hi?
Naw—I'll walk on by

I don't smoke so I'm above ... right?
I lost more than her love that night

She said, "baby," & kept on grinnin'
Double the crack ... that ain't winnin'

at 5 am before the sun
someone called nine-one-one

They tried oh, so tough
but she'd had her last puff

When Medic One took her
no lights overhead

They knew Ms. Ann was
brain dead

Five pm, it was for real
her death they revealed

I cried without reason why
I didn't want Ms. Ann to die

I thought I could have intervened
Now I see what it means

If I had crossed that street
I might have had a maker to meet

Ms. Ann can't cry where she's at
and my heart has to accept that

At 53, there's another way
to hold on for a new day

Ms. Ann for 17 hours chose crack ...
I cried, but I can come back ...

—*Roxane Roberts*

THIS CHOICE ... MY ONLY CHOICE

Integrity made this choice

My actions have a voice

in this asphalt cocoon

where there is never a moon

Dreams battered and distorted

love so fleeting and sordid

I wake up and change you see

because my dreams are made by me!

—*Roxane Roberts*

SHADOW SURVIVORS

Proud Americans
Stepping up to donate
Food
   Clothing
      Shelter
         Cash
            Jobs
To those recently made homeless by
        Hurricane Katrina

The same Americans who have
   Shunned
      Ignored
         Derided
The homeless in their midst for decades

Right now in this Great Land
Drift the shadow survivors of Invisible Katrinas
Storms of life that have blown them astray

Six shadows standing behind each face on the news
Now forced to wait even longer for help
As the recent victims supplant them in the aid lines

When you open your hearts and purses
to those you see in the media
Remember the six shadows in your own hometown
Victims of the Invisible Katrinas
Must not be left behind

—*Reneene Robertson*

FIRE HOARDER

Third and Prefontaine
Comes a man
With cigarette in hand
"Do you have a light?"
Asks he

With a dirty look
The man
Shakes his head
Shuts him down
Climbs aboard the bus
Headed uptown

Turning then he spies
A woman
"Do you have a match?"
He asks
"I don't smoke"
Her curt reply

Shoulders slump
Reluctant hand
Reaches into pocket
Brings out matchbook

Sacrificing
One future fire
From his dwindling supply
He fills his nicotine need now

Sensing the
Silent laughter
Behind him
He walks on

—*Reneene Robertson*

HOBO STEW

Hobo Stew
More than a meal
A lesson for us all
If we share with others
Even when we can't afford to
The resulting mix can be delicious
And nourishing for all

—Reneene Robertson

MYSTICS GO TO THE MOUNTAINS

Mystics go
  To the mountains
    Because
Having visions
  In the City
Can get you
  Beat up
      and
    Locked up

—Reneene Robertson

Pitching a fit
At mental health professionals
Is chancy at best

—*Reneene Robertson*

Imaginary friends
Keeping busy
At the mental health clinic

—*Reneene Robertson*

WORDS

Words
Sculpting phrases
Stringing screaming syllables
Now this pattern
Now that
So many choices

Words
Drag me from under
  my warm blanket
Demanding life
Dancing thru my mind
Dreams forgotten

Words
Grab me
Rule me
Have made me their slave
Write
  They insist
Write now
  So I do

—*Reneene Robertson*

UNITED URBAN NATION

Everyday is United Nations Day
On the streets

Walking . . . Walking . . . Walking

Be careful where you choose
To rest your weary feet
You might be arrested if you
Sit down in the wrong places
Gaze into the wrong faces

Weaving through the crowds
of Shoppers
of Workers
of "real" People

Invisible to all but each other
are the United Nations
of this country's urban cores

Living in this Nation
yet not a part of it
Living nowhere and everywhere

Ignored
Disregarded
Discarded

Invisible to all but each other
Our United Urban Nations

—*Reneene Robertson*

THE MEEK

The meek shall inherit the earth
And I hope we can do it in time
Yes the meek shall inherit the earth
But I hope by the time that we do
It's worth more than a dime

—*Reneene Robertson*

URBAN HAIKU

We gave our children
Nothing worth living for
Now they die for nothing

—*Reneene Robertson*

CONVERSATIONS

Walking down the street
Alone
Talking out loud

Having
Imaginary conversations
With
Real People

Is
This only
The first step
To having
Real conversations
With
Imaginary people
?

—Reneene Robertson

PEOPLE ARE DREAMERS

People are dreamers
    and people are dreams
And the dreams are the dreamers
    and the dreamers are dreams

In the streams of your mind
    in the mists of your soul
You must be both
    ere you will not be whole

Not all of life's dreams
    need to hide from the light
Not all of life's dreams
    need to wait for the night

When the dreams are the dreamers
    and the dreamers the dreams
All the shards of reality
    melt in life's streams

And they ebb and they flow
    'til you finally know
Which dreams must live
    and which dreams must go

—Reneene Robertson

HEAD TRIP

Hop on . . . take a ride
Take a ride deep down inside
'Round and 'round and down we go
To the psyche far below

Down below the street facade
Where things are real
      where things are odd
Down where all the true selves dwell
Where each one has a tale to tell

Down below the hurtful shells
Of Pain and Fear and private hells
To the glowing central core
Where Peace and Love bathe every shore

And in that loving peaceful tide
A quiet place where we can bide
A place to rest awhile and then
We'll spiral up and out again

To face once more the world outside
Strengthened by our inner guide
Knowing we can go below
When e'er we need our peace to flow

—Reneene Robertson

CREATIVITY
(in two parts)

Without the madness
The creativity
Would not function

Without the creativity
The madness
Would be unbearable

—Reneene Robertson

HOW LONG ?

How long can I push myself
   Until I drop or die ?

How long will I have to go
   Before I reach the sky ?

And when I reach it will I know
   When I have gone too high

Or will I look around
   And realize I've learned to fly
     Oh my

—*Reneene Robertson*

TREE FRIEND

A tree friend is a true friend
My tree friend saved my life one night
    many years ago

    "GO"
        "DANGER"
            "RUN"
She cried out in my mind

Her warning made me faster than
The man lurking behind her

Last week I returned to thank her
I sat on her stump
        and cried

—*Reneene Robertson*

THE RAINBOW BARRETTE

I was three
My grandma gave me
A rainbow barrette
I liked it a lot
It looked pretty
In my dark hair

One day while playing
Outside at our apartments
I lost it
Left behind in
The scary zone

It wasn't scary all the time
Only when the "Wolf Pack" ran
School time was safe time

I didn't know
How to tell time with clocks
The sun told me
When the safe times were

The sun said "short but safe"
So I hurried back for my
Rainbow barrette

It sparkled in the sun
I had just picked it up
When I saw them

My surprise delayed
Prevented
My escape
Daylight saving didn't save me

—Reneene Robertson

MY FIRST MURDER

How I hated you that day
Miss Priss
Miss Perfect
With your perfect hair
And your perfect family
With your money
With your superior attitude

How I wanted to make you hurt
Pain so bad
Kicking your ass
Would not be enough agony
I had to hurt you more

I had to kill the one person
In all the world
Who meant the most to you
Who loved you
Who brought you presents
And was magic too

My rage put murder in my heart
So I did it
I killed him

"Santa's not real"
I hissed
"He's just your parents"

I could see on your face
That I had drawn blood
I thrust the killing blow
"Go ask your mom"

You did

The pain and grief
In both pair of eyes
Pierced my soul

I
Will
Never
Kill
Again

—Reneene Robertson

THE UFO

Daddy   look !
  Do you see that ?
    What is that ?
    What makes it go ?
      Why does it smell like that?
Where is it taking Mommy ?
        Daddy
            Daddy
  Why are you crying ?

—Reneene Robertson

GRANDMOTHER SPIDER

Grandmother Spider
Showed me her
Web

Time
Swirling
Spiraling
into
Tomorrow / Yesterday

Myth perceptions
Clear up the
Past / Future

Galaxies
Light up the
Universal Dance

All connected

Each act
Each word
Each thought

Plucks the strings
Vibrating the whole web

Recreating
Creation
Moment by moment
Forever

—*Reneene Robertson*

CITY PARK

Huge shared living room
  Living carpet
    Tiny things
Living in the living carpet
    Baby laughter
  Soaring above crow conversations
    Crows soaring over
     Laughing babies
Land traffic
  Air traffic
    Blend with
     Siren accents
Urban music fades and swells
  Drum circle heartbeats
    Keeping it all alive

—Reneene Robertson

HAIKU

Shell-shocked soldiers
share solitary cells
in the prison of their souls.

—Reneene Robertson

TENT CITY SOUND (NIGHT)

The nightingale's song is a siren,
A parking lot light the moon.
Tent zippers are crickets,
Sliding into my warm cocoon.
To the left a baby crying,
Snoring on my right.
Now I wish for sleep,
To the sounds of a
Tent City night.

—Jennifer R.

CARRYING A SIGN

Leaves on the wind
Circle in the air
Frantic warnings
Emissaries from a wiser world

No one heeds them
People push toward
Their usual destinations
In their everyday faces

The leaves make the street wonderful
Without them it would be entirely
Devoted to business and I would feel like dying
 I would have to walk up and down
Carrying a sign
"Bring Back The Leaves"

—Elizabeth Romero

LOVE, A PROSE POEM

And suddenly she realized that there would always be those who laughed at love, who sneered at it, who mocked it, tried to make it something fleeting and negligible like an itch, and those who believed in it, in its mystical power, its purity, its inability to do wrong, its power to heal — against all evidence, against all odds.

And all the time love would move among them, touching unbelievers and believers alike, the way the buttery sun of springtime touches soft-cheeked laughing toddlers in the park and also flows over a sleeping tramp — dark and grizzled — illuminating the weave of his jacket, the skin beneath his stubbled beard — love, incorruptible and kind, moves among us always.

—Elizabeth Romero

IT SEEMS TO ME

It seems to me
the world bows down with the weight
of lonely people

A divorced man drinks in his room
haunted by memories too painful to admit
of his racing rain-splashed youth

It seems to me men and women are cut off
from the changing light of day
in cubicles,
in the dark hidden halls
of bright chain restaurants

The world bows down
with the weight of lonely people
going back each day
and coming out again

day follows day
with its collection
of bright and dark hours

I know, I know: I can hear you say
lonely people are lucky
to be just lonely
and not crippled
blind
maimed
mad

—*Elizabeth Romero*

ON THE OTHER HAND

I believe it is love alone
That impels us
In the indifferent universe
Bright furless creatures
With naked hands and eyes

I walk at night
After the rain
I pull on the branches
To feel the cold drops
Scuff through the leaves
I don't want to get old
I don't want to die

When I look inside myself
I see longing for lasting joy
And to be someone who loves
But also I would like to have a gold wristwatch
And be young and slim again

—*Elizabeth Romero*

ORDINARY DAY

And then on one perfectly ordinary day
We walked out of the house which had been
As solid beneath our feet as stone
And as silent
We never came back
We learned that on one perfectly ordinary day
Life can change forever

—Elizabeth Romero

SLOW EROSIONS

It's October now.
The sky is lemon yellow.
It's cold enough to keep the door closed.
The leaves are falling faster.
Something inside me rushes forward
                                    when I watch them.
They flash downward like signals.

There have been so many partings,
so many slow erosions.
It all goes so fast.
Night falls; the leaves
sweep along the neighborhood streets.

I miss you. I love you.
I never loved you enough.

I want to be unafraid like the leaves.
Flutter my flutter; flash my flash.
Plummet downward seized by the wind.
Make room for the night and the cold.

—*Elizabeth Romero*

THESE ARE OUR DREAMS

Above these dark suburban streets
The stars come out like children
One by one
The moon is like a mask of tragedy
She is like a white heart
Beating in cloud's ribs

Christmas is just past
And the silent lights twinkle
In each small yard: a pine tree, a snowman

Inside a woman in a kitchen bends towards the sink,
a television illuminates a dark room

On the lawn a fat red-suited elf
With magic reindeer and the holy family:
A woman, a man and a baby in the clothing of a place
Half a world away these are our dreams

The ancient Celts, the North Pole, Palestine

Where Christmas began
Where we clung together against the darkness
Where magically poor children got what they wanted
Where the Son of Man was born
And we were taught to love and to give

Here in the suburbs it is very dark
Every driveway has two chariots
With hate on the bumpers
And greed in the tanks

—*Elizabeth Romero*

UNTITLED

I think of the spider.
She throws out her line
out and out, again and again.
But when I try to sail out on my own line
the basic signposts fail.
The world hums and hisses
with the question and the silence,
a bird's wind, the center of a flower
illuminated.
I hear the cats move
with their soft scrabble.
From somewhere I hear the yip of a dog,
the slam of a car door,
voices too far away for meaning.
In here, the refrigerator clears its throat,
a preliminary to conversation
that never begins.
The big red chair is faded,
staunch, sagging like a skid row hotel, The voices cease, the silence deepens.
The plant in the window is crooked as a question mark
blossoming into leaves.
And the question is sharp and deep
as the stillness of the night.

—*Elizabeth Romero*

COLORED CARNATIONS

Like a chick that has made
her first crack in the rigid eggshell
that once protected her,
I have begun my awakening.

Senses unblocked
by once solid layers of anxiety
pieces of sky, blue light
now shine through
and I notice my world more.

Multi-colored carnations
grace my kitchen with their spicy smells
and festive flames of color:
orange, fuchsia, pink, yellow,
red, purple and white.
Coming together to look like
the crepe-paper on a Mexican pinata.

On arriving home I see them
when I first open my door.
In a few seconds,
sight is joined by smell
as their fragrance wafts over to me.

Delighted to be able
to make their acquaintance,
I talk to each blossom
giving them my appreciation for being there.
My talk with them isn't that linear,
it's more like cutesy baby talk,
words just for the two of us,

For a long time,
sensual was too close to sexual,
and sexual was too close to fear.
And fear stood guard and
kept erect those rigid sides of my eggshell wall.
When you're not ready yet,
still a chick curled in a shell,
it's hard to know how easy it would be
to turn your head and peck through.

And you don't know then that you will like it
or that just around the corner,
a sun-brightened bouquet of carnations
is coming to dance like breeze-tossed mariposas *
doing the minuet on your windowsill.

*Spanish word for butterfly

—K. Maia Rose

CONNECTIONS

I live my life as a filament
like a tiny piece of narrow string.
In the holographic universe of quantum physics
the smallest of the smallest elements of matter
are said to be like strings*
infinitesimally tiny, double, pretzel-twisted loops of string-shaped stuff.
You and me, they and them, and those over there
all of us sharing at the microcosmic level
the same kind of small, stringy stuff.

I breathe in air, you breathe in air,
sometimes we breathe in each others air.
Air molecules containing atoms
with quarks, particles, waves,
even tiny bits of cellular structure
that once surrounded the dust motes in Plato's kitchen
become part of us, things brand new,
and things a million years old swirling around inside
with vast stretches of interval space.

I live my life as a filament
like a tiny piece of narrow string
and my strings are strung over to your strings
and at some level you and I
and we and they are all connected.
All perfectly ordinary aspects of this one thing called life.

If I string up a guitar and sing a tune
my song could be your song
and your song could be my song
and all songs could be one song
that we all sing in unison,
right out loud, and unashamed.
Because beneath it all
we are all tiny, little loops of string
quivering, vibrating, humming the same old ho-hum story
looking to rest our heads on the same old ho-hum bed
relaxed and without tension.

I live my life as a filament
like a tiny piece of narrow string.
An ordinary woman strung with ordinary strings
breathing ordinary air connected to your ordinary air.
When there is tension tugging on my strings
a corresponding tension plucks at your strings too
because in many ways we are one
and at the same time many more than one.
We are ordinary life; every woman and every man.

I live my life as a filament
like a tiny piece of narrow string.

In quantum physics "string theory" is based on a mathematical formula.

—*K. Maia Rose*

I AM GOING TO TALK

I am going to leave
this area someday
I am going to travel.
I am not going to stay put
I am going to be on the move.
I am already preparing to go,
clearing out my head space,
moving things around
so that I can travel light.

And I am going to talk.
I am going to talk about
what happened to me
talk and talk and talk
until all of those who
need this talk
find a home in me.

I am not going to stay put
I am not going to hold still
I am not going to be good
I am not going to be silent.
I am going to travel
and tell everyone what's
inside of me until it's
inside of you too.

—*K. Maia Rose*

LET ME BE

Let me be hard, tough, grisled, unfeeling
I have no need of love or joy
Give me a quarter towards another pack of smokes
The rush of nicotine is as close as I want to get towards
        feeling something

Let me be enclosed in my hard, impenetrable shell
Don't seek to make me laugh or cry
Don't wake my heart, I prefer to let it sleep
Let me be content with existence, anything more is only
        asking for heartache

Passions can only be afforded by the rich
Where can a homeless woman go to fall apart in tears?
Would you pity me or despise me if I stood on a street
        corner allowing my emotions to stream?
You would cluck your tongue in a disgusted way and
        comment on the
fact that the homeless "are just everywhere today"

Homelessness is brokenness

If one opens her eyes and heart to beauty, she must also
    acknowledge the pain of broken dreams
Pain is something I have a wellspring full of
I can't afford to acknowledge all the losses: comfort,
    security, dignity, hopes for the future
Because even though I'm broken, I still must take my place
    on the street corners, unable
to hide my feelings from a world that couldn't care any less
    than it already does

Let me immerse myself in my world
Let me be oblivious to your world so that I may be free of
    constant longing
Let me be stripped of awareness
Let me be cold, unemotional, expressionless
On second thought, just let me be.

—*Claire R. Rowe*

HOME IS

For some
Home is a house
      or an apartment
For others
Home is a tent
      or a doorway
For the rest
Home is being in one's element
Where people are
      respectful
      honest
      real
Where talent is encouraged
Pain is shared
Joy is rare and special
Where people are what you see
Where who you are is accepted —

My home on the street.

—Paula Rozner

JUST KEEP WALKING

your head aches
your stomach growls
        just keep walking

throat parched
mouth dry
        just keep walking

stomach hurts
head pounds
        just keep walking

vision blurs
sounds are senseless
        just keep walking

muscles weaken
whole body hungers
        just keep walking

road weaves
moves under feet
        just keep walking

there's a park
maybe some rest
            cop comes
        just keep walking

a dollar please
a burger to eat
        just keep walking

body hurts
sit for a moment
            cop comes
        just keep walking

—*Paula Rozner*

IF I HAD WINGS

If I had wings with which to fly.
I would soar up into the Big Blue Sky,
If I had a song I'd sing it loud,
and make the lord so very proud,
If I had a way to make this world better,
I would snap my fingers
and make it soft as a feather.
If I had wings I'd fly you away
from all this hurt and pain.

—Christina R.

LADY IN WAITING

Tossing, turning, bed too hot, too hard
Not time to get up yet
Waiting ...
Sitting & reading the paper, friends haven't arrived
Not time for breakfast yet
Waiting...
Standing & checking the schedule, mind drifting
Not time for the bus yet
Waiting ...
Can't go anywhere, bags too heavy
Not time for laundry yet
Waiting ...
Exhausted, achy, dying for a nap
Not time to come in yet
Waiting ...

I am a lady-in-waiting
I wait for food
I wait to bathe
I wait to travel
I wait to sleep
I'm so tired of waiting, waiting for my life to return

—*Nancy S.*

SIGHT

Touching him through touching me
White haired, painted face witch doctor.
His breath on my face
alternates with a medicine stick.

Silence brings forth a gale
stance shaken.
Cold air surrounds me
Feet still connected to earth.

Spirit elder backs away
eyes and medicine stick threatening
but with a look of fear.
His magic useless on me.

Momentary darkness
gray wolf approaches
slow thoughtful strides
stopping gaze connecting

Touching him through touching me
His visions returning my sight.

—*Marta Sanchez*

THIS HOUSE CALLED HOME

Through the door
heart in pieces
breathing deeply
sensing life
beginnings and
endings
A leap of faith into
this house called home.
Trembling
struggling
choking on fear
arms unfolding
bathing the pain
in love
acceptance
recognition
Healing
first steps
stumbling, falling
time and again
get up
get up

listening, feeling
blushing
hiding
come out
try again
together we'll walk
Paths winding
footsteps firm
embracing
acknowledging
living, loving
fluttering sorrows
soaring with eagles
into the creator's arms
Shattered glass
into smooth silhouette
vases of life
holding treasures
of
this house called home.

—Kris Schon

FOR ELLEN

Today, I saw the first autumn leaf
On the birch tree
Outside my window
Premature
like the way you died.

I want this to be
Just a zen test,
another therapeutic technique
You will come back from
To see how I'd react.
Now it's alchemy
From a textbook
Without words.

I am the arborist
But you worked on the spirit
In the tree;
Peeling away layers of bark
Exposing the smooth, new wood
Underneath.
sometime there are fears
In the form of weevils
Trying to bore their way to the
heart;

But there's an application of pitch-tar
to heal the wounds until the
sweet, sticky sap comes to the surface
flowing, metamorphosizing
into amber-hued jewels
I can later burn as incense
To relive in ceremony
Our work:

> Restoring vigor to this tree
> So it may let the wind pass through
> Unfettered.
> So many generations of ravens
> Will come to play
> In its life
> So many eyes will continue
> To witness
> The beauty of it all.

I wanted to hold on to you
Longer,
But you are the movement
Of the fog itself
Holding moon's illumination
In a cold, dark night.

—*Lynn Sereda*

UNTITLED

"All the flowers of all the tomorrows
are in the seeds of today" – Chinese proverb

How do moments like this disappear
Yet remain timeless?
Holding hands in the arboretum
A waft of breeze; pollen dusts my hair
Pheromones singing in
Warm humid air
Locked in embrace
Under Torreya Californica
I still remember the tree

We were gong to grow plants together
Instead of children.
Create food, medicine and
Sacred Botanica.
Now, I'm alone, just
Trying to create myself.

Across the world
A lotus unfolds
Sturdy petals
Out from the unadmired muck.

—*Lynn Sereda*

TEARDROPS

As my teardrops touch my eyes then fall to my face, yes don't feel bad for me, because I can get out all my hurt, only God knows how much pain.

Thank you for your love, respect, understanding. Thank you for letting me be me.

—*Margaret Shaw*

LIGHTNING

slashes of white-hot rage
stabbing the tender sky
with silent daggers

—*Janice Shivers*

THE QUILT

She knows it isn't long before
she must leave to go
live on the streets, as she
packs away a lifetime's belongings
soon to be hers no longer.

She picks up the last item, a quilt.
A glorious, patchwork quilt
patiently stitched by loving hands
generations ago. She holds it
reverently, with trembling hands.

And remembers bouncing up and
down on it on her parent's bed
during those childhood days
of bright promise.

She thinks about her bridal shower,
when her mother presented it to her
enjoining them in an age-old tradition
from mother to child
now a woman, soon to
be a wife lying upon it
with her husband.

And the memories of their
countless nights spent
entwined as two young trees
whose branches have grown
together
take hold of her once again.

Then walking out the door,
she wonders how the quilt's maker would feel
seeing her gathered tightly in it
seeking warmth for the body
and emotional strength from
the auras it carries
of generations past.

—*Janice Shivers*

TO ALL BUT GOD

When you see me
you see only

a fat Indian
an ugly woman

a too young mother
a shabby dresser

When you hear me
you hear only

a toothy lisp
a faltering memory

a too talkative loner
a frustrated yell

If you delve a little deeper
you'll find

poor health — a drain to health care
two kids — a drain to welfare
mental illness — a drain to the sane

You'll never know the beautiful child
who loved to dress up as a princess

or the dynamic grad speaker
who had the crowd on its feet

or the vibrant bride full of hope
for a lifelong partner in love

to you I remain
pitiful, worthless, unlovable
— to all but God

You think I don't see your arrogant sneer
don't hear you hostile snicker

as I lug groceries and kids
and my own swollen body

on buses, through malls
across busy streets

I keep my eyes down
but my head up

I turn stone deaf
to the jagged slurs

I choke back a tear
and keep my mouth shut

now my pain becomes visceral
it cannot be hidden

so I can dance like St. Vitas
and draw more stares still

I'm reminded of how I must seem
how pathetic, how odd

I can't prove my beauty
—to any but God.

—Heather S.
(Reprinted from *Our Voice*, Edmonton, Alberta)

MAN ABOUT TOWN

When you meet a man about town
A man of the world, with bedroll and worn out shoes
There are some things you must not say.
Don't speak about warm satin floors
Your new espresso machine
Or the doors you use to shut out the world.
He longs for your privacy
Dreams of nothing on his back but
the effortless air.

—*Liz Smith*

OPEN SEASON

When the police
Shoot their bullets
Between empty upraised hands
Straight into the devastated heart
Of an unarmed black man
And the blood flows like a moon-pulled tide
They stand together
Each resting one careless foot on the corpse
Puffing happily on cigars
They slap each other on the back
And celebrate
Showing all their teeth.

—*Liz Smith*

THE QUIET MAN

The quiet man
Bows to the wind
Like a weeping willow on a soft fall evening.
He sleeps in seclusion
On the hard ground, on the yielding grasses
Of the great plains
Under the stars, light-years away.
The quiet man shivers
In apprehension.
Winter will soon come
Bringing the hard winds, unceasing rain, and
gloomy clouds
Each dawn a fresh grey misery.
No one sees the quiet man, not even God,
Who sees every sparrow
But, apparently, not the suffering
Of the quiet man
Who passes like a shadow
Along the grimy streets,
Each day he lessens
Like a skeletal tree, leaves gusted away one by one
All good things falling away
Never to be seen again.
The quiet man
Never quite gives up
Never gets a lucky break
In a better world
The quiet man
Sits in a rocking chair
Holding a grandchild on his lap
Reading Goodnight Moon
While a tall clock ticks softly in the hall
And a wine-dark stew simmers on the stove.

This poem is so useless
I am so helpless
I could write until the world ends
Give my tears, promise devotion,
And it wouldn't bring about even one brick
To shelter the quiet man
Who once had a future
And a loving family.
Close your eyes, and
Dream along with me.

—*Liz Smith*

TWO DISHEVELED SOULS GET TO MEET GOD EVEN THOUGH THEIR HAIR IS A MESS

A woman with shabby bundles on her back
Holds her little daughter's hand
As they trudge east up a mountain road, towards Pakistan.
The child looks up, points
At yellow boxes falling from a grey sky.
"Mama, pretty, look!" cries the child.
She thinks they are December birds.

The boxes sing no song.
The boxes tick softly to themselves
Backwards... 10... 9... 8... 7...
Two new souls are flying up to Heaven.

In Heaven there is no pain, no tears.
There is perfect love.
All voices sing in perfect pitch
No matter what the words.

—*Liz Smith*

BE NOT AFRAID LITTLE ONES,
JUST LOOK UP TO THE SKY.

Be not afraid little ones
as that dark blanket of night comes down.
You may be homeless
but there's nothing to fear,
as long as you look up
as you drift off to sleep.
Just look up and watch the clouds
there's magic within,
If you use your imagination
magic angels will appear
watching over you as you sleep.
You can even count them as they dance past
In the heavens above.
Be not afraid little ones
for when you look up there's a caring grace,
that keeps all children safe
as that dark blanket comes down.

This's my prayer for you
that you will always look up,
the magic that keeps you safe
will always tuck you in.

This's for those of you that have lost
your homes to a fire
or just moving into your next,
as long as you look up
there's nothing to fear.

—*Belinda A. Springer*

PATCHWORK QUILT

Staring at a patchwork quilt
  the square patterns
    lead around, and around
Like the streets that form
  Similar blocked patterns
    of this city
We all call home.

As I stare at the blocks, with
  all the weaves of strands
    of yarn, I see the same
      patterns within the people
        walking around the blocks
          weaving in between, the
            cracks between doorways
            and alleys in this city.
Sometimes it seems as if
  no one really knows
    they're there, woven
      between the strands
        of buildings that fill
          our city

You know, it's cold out there,
  as I look at the patterns of
    this quilt ...

—*Belinda A. Springer*

FEAR

Fear can make us act hasty.
It can twist us until we go crazy or,
don't know what direction to go or
don't care. When you live in fear
It seems that's all you know.
The wounds of hate-filled words scar
the very center of children's hearts,
Who don't understand why Mom is always crying!

—Storm

SOCIOLOGY OF SOCIETY

Sociology of society controlling me.
Morbid moralists, moralizing me.
In this shriek and siege reality.

Trying to abolish humanity, abusing society,
with politics straining success.
Fuck the stipulations of politicians,
discrediting society.

With poverty all around
the loss of employment's growing fast,
shelters are closed down.

You've done your share of taking
when will you give some back ...
to family values.

You left my proof of innocence
sitting upon the shelves in the Court of Appeals.

—Storm

AT THE CROSSROADS
(Following the attacks on America, September 11, 2001)

We
watch
in shock
as planes hit
as buildings fall
as countless people die.
People cry (too fast!)
for vengeance —
but war will not heal us.
More pain
cannot heal us.
Only hope
can
heal.

—Ria Strong

I NEVER REALLY HAD YOU

You say you feel you're losing me.
You say that I disown you.
You say you just can't reach me.
You say you'll always miss me.

You say you feel you're losing me;
I, too, have known pain.
   (Where were you?)
You say that I disown you;
I've known betrayals too great for words.
   (Where were you?)
You say you just can't reach me;
I've known a rage I dared not face.
   (Where were you?)
You say you'll always miss me;
I've known despair too deep for tears.
   (Where were you?)

You say you feel you're losing me;
I know I never had you.

—*Ria Strong*

JUST TWO QUESTIONS ...

I.
Why did the cleaners
who found me unconscious
at the tram stop
on Swanston Street—
why did those cleaners
call the police
for help?

2.
The police.
when they came—
why did they
smell my breath
What is she?
Drunk?
and check my arms
for needle tracks
before wondering if maybe,
just maybe,
I was sick?

—Ria Strong

SWIMMING

Cutting
through the water,
up and down the lap lane
I swim; my friends paddle in the
shallows.

On land,
my left leg drags
and my hand curls, awkward;
in the water, my spastic limbs
are strong.

—*Ria Strong*

GENESIS AND EXODUS

hibernating, homesteading in my small
one-person cave of existence in claimed
remote territory of the world,
receiving visitors rarely unless they reeked of
the familiar aroma of darkness or despair.
awakening, slowly, one Spring to the
presence of intruders who somehow
eluded my built-in security alarm system
catching me with guard down
captivated me with tales of
travels abroad to unknown worlds of joy
and happiness open even to such as I
stirring up within me newfound desire and boldness
to venture forth from the comforts of my home.
they, alternately leading, pushing,
gently prodding, supporting.
I, sporadically balking, walking,
retreating, frolicking through
these strange new lands of freedom and liberty.
pining sometimes for the familiarity of my past abode
yet knowing that I can not, must not, will not
return to live in that grave ever again.

—TC

CANNED BONED CHICKEN

I got one pack of Bugler
And a twelve pack of beer
I'm gonna sit down
And make me a meal
I'll have to get me this box
Just my lucky day
Canned boned chicken, USDA
Twelve cans in the box
Packed in water
I don't know —
Do you think a oughta?

It fell down by the tracks
and it fell my way
Canned boned chicken, USDA
It's my lucky day
It fell right here
Gonna pop me a can
And drink me a beer
Gonna roll me a Bugler
And open up the box of —
Canned boned chicken, USDA

Gettin down to picken with my P38
Picken around with my P38
Canned boned chicken, USDA
Canned boned chicken, USDA
I'm gonna do some smokin'
And get down to drinkin'
I'm gonna do some finger pickin'
I'm gonna do some finger lickin'
I'm gonna sit down and make me a meal
Canned boned chicken and a can of beer

Canned boned chicken, USDA
Fell off the tracks

It's my luck today
Doin' some smokin', drinkin' and chicken picken'
12 cans-canned boned chicken
Fell to me feet, this lucky day
Canned boned chicken, USDA
Canned boned chicken, USDA
Canned boned chicken, USDA
Chicken Pickin!

—*Grace B.T.*

VIEW AT JOSE RIZAL PARK

*Jose Rizal Park is a park on Beacon Hill
overlooking Seattle, Washington*

He walked to the park
took his chicken out,
began to wash before dinner,
the sun set over the Olympics
as he washed his hands
for five full minutes,
then he rinsed
his store bought chicken,
knees bent sitting
on his haunches
like old Vietnamese villagers,
he watched the sun's
last lavender light
slip into darkness
over the Sound,
his utensils rested
on his back pack,
his face forever brown,
unnatural for his race,
his teeth white straight,
he was a man
with no shelter
for the night,
no matter,
he ate off a plastic plate,
counted himself lucky
with his fresh fruit and grains,
an art park scene floated nearby,
a short dark girl goes by
walking her tall white dog,
a chubby African boy
giggles on a swing,

and he feels lucky to be
counted again among the living,
safe, clean and warm,
human rays have replaced the sun
smiles all around,
he knows he'll rest soon
to rise once more
off the cold mother earth floor
to look for work downtown
by the Millionair's Club,
once a name for swanky swells,
now a place for men
who need a day job,
to push the hunger away,
whet the whistle:
brown men, white men, black men,
sober drunks, men with a record,
illegal aliens, students of mine,
from Mexico, Guatemala, Honduras,
protected by an unwritten clause within the city,
allowing corporate welfare,
local independent contractors, restauranteurs
to benefit under the table.

—*Angie Vasquez*

WHITE WASHER PLANT TOWN

When he was young
and growing up in that
white washer plant town,
he was scared
because "they" said,
"Them nuclear bombs
out there can kill ya,
so y'all better beware
and buy this here bomb shelter,
plant it in your back yard,
if'n you got one,
to protect you and yours,
from the nuclear fear fallout
from the goddamn KGB commies
before they be knocking down
the USA Corporate door with their
anti-capitalist red scare tactics,
with one touch of the button
they'll blow your house down,
you know they will."
Well, those farmers, Maytag-ers,
but not the one-armed railroaders
bought them up in a flash,
his little brown boy thought was,
"Shit, what about us?
Who'll take care of us?
We'll die out here."

—*Angie Vasquez*

BE YOURSELF

I won't grovel at your feet or act like you want me to.
Being a woman I do what I want to do.
I'm a happy person
I smile at most everyone I met.
I'll stop and talk and joke around with friends on the street

I do it all the time
That's my trademark

Basically people are good
Given ideas or advice just being friendly and kind

But never, never lose sight of your own mind
Respect it

O yes in my life there is sadness, disappointment and hurt
but I stop, take a big sigh and say it could have been worse

And keep on keeping on!
So, be proud of who you are

Be what you want to be
Because I'm sure going to be me

—*Estella Wallace*

SLEEPING OUTDOORS

Homeless people have a hard time sleeping outdoors. They lose their jobs and then their home and there's nowhere to go when the money is gone. Tired and sick but what can you do, friends can't help — they're hurting too. Homeless people have a hard time sleeping outdoors.

Too many shot and killed on the street — some dear souls while they're asleep, sleeping under bridges, doorways, and sheds, cardboard boxes for a bed. Plastic bags to carry their all and no place to go when nature calls. Homeless people have a hard time sleeping outdoors.

Turned away when the shelters are filled, but offered a blanket and minus a meal. Told good luck — you're on your own, under the viaduct hungry and cold with one eye open and one eye closed. Homeless people have a hard time sleeping outdoors.

Most homeless people really try, work every day for smaller pay. But let me set the record straight cause there's been too many lies and too much hate. Called bums for just being poor, they fought the wars when you and me were scared to go. They served their country for honor and peace, some lost their lives for you and me. Homeless people have a hard time sleeping outdoors.

—Estella Wallace

I'M A BRAT

I'm a brat
I freely admit it
Not proud of it
But thought I should fess up

I have a thin skin
and forget others have feelings
I stopped smiling
and let everyone see a side of me
I'd rather not show

Later I'm sorry
but it's too late
They've gone, left with an impression
of a grouchy, middle-aged woman

It may be that I feel
time is passing by too quickly
I don't have the time
to make sure everyone else is okay
I've become selfish

I'm lost
   in the sea of what I should
     and should not do
Of what is proper
   and what is not
Everywhere I turn, a different answer

I need a break
from smiling, teaching, working, worrying—
I need a warm hug
   then a firm push

Send me out and let me be!
Take care of things
   while I'm gone
And maybe when I return
   I can smile
     and mean it

—*Margi Washburn*

THE WOMEN OF WHEEL AND FRIENDS IN ACTION

Sheryl Barlia

WHEEL Valentines Day Rally 1997

Catherine Condeff

Janice Connelly

WHEEL Valentines Day Rally, 1997

Penny Boggs writing at Tent City, 2000

Jean Dawson

"Black Beauty"

With Seattle Mayor Paul Schell at Seattle Center, 2000

Madeline Lewis

Marion Sue Fischer

Michele and Anitra at Tent City, 2000

Women in Black vigil, 2006

Mona Joyner

Cynthia Ozimek

Women in Black *vigil*

Stations of the Cross, Westlake Mall, 2003

Vivian Nelson

Women cleaning the Bunk House

Janice Connelly

Anitra L. Freeman

WHEEL Valentines Day Rally 1997

*Reneene Robertson
and Arnette Adams at
The Womens Forum,
2006*

Women in Black *vigil, outside Seattle Justice Center, 2006*

COLOPHON

The cover title type is OPTIAmadeus, OPTIGibby and Helvetica Neue. Cover image by Eva Serrabassa of iStockphoto. Back cover images are from Jean Schweitzer of iStockphoto and "Black Beauty" photo is from the WHEEL photo archives. The interior images are gleaned from a variety of image banks, adapted for use by the designer, or courtesy of the WHEEL archives. Photographers are (in alphabetical order) Flo Beaumon, Carol C., Tish Colston, Elise DeGooyer, Sinan Demirel, Julie Eagleton, Michele Marchand, and WHEEL members.

The interior headline type is set in Helvetica Neue, a font evolving from the original Helvetica designed by Max Miedinger in 1957. The name Helvetica is derived from the Roman name for Switzerland. It is based on the earlier Akzidenz Grotesk typeface (originally titled Haas-Grotesk) from around 1898. Helvetica became extremely popular in the 1960s and in 1983 Linotype released a retooling called Helvetica Neue (German for "New Helvetica") used here. The cover OPTI fonts were developed and digitized by the Kreiter family of Castcraft Software, a close-knit family type foundry doing business since 1936. The interior text blocks were set in AGaramond from Adobe Type. AGaramond is a recasting of the classic serif type face Garamond, originally designed in the 16th century by Claude Garamond. AGaramond was designed by Robert Slimbach in 1989.

Interior stock is 60# recycled. with 30%, post consumer recycled content. Cover stock is recycled 80# Utopia II (10% PCW), coated one side only with lay-flat matt film lamination.

Book design by Tracy Lamb, Laughing Lamb Design, Jackson Hole, Wyoming. Print production by Sheridan Books, Inc. of Chelsea, Michigan.

PERMISSIONS & COPYRIGHTS

All the poems in this anthology were previously published by WHEEL in chapbooks issued in conjunction with our annual Homeless Women's Forums. Each individual woman retains the copyright to her own work. Every effort was made to contact each poet selected for this anthology. To protect their privacy, WHEEL has used the first name and last initial of some poets we could not locate.

We would love to hear from any of the WHEEL poets we could not contact; corrections can be made in reprints.

Some women feel shame about being homeless. The women of WHEEL strongly believe that the shame lies in a system that allows homelessness to exist, not with the individuals who experience it.

—The Women of WHEEL

ABOUT WHIT PRESS

Empowering Community through the Literary Arts

Whit Press is a nonprofit publishing organization dedicated to the transformational power of the written word.

Whit Press exists to nurture and promote the rich diversity of literary work from women writers, writers from ethnic and social minorities, young writers, and first-time authors.

We also create books that use literature as a tool in support of other nonprofit organizations working toward environmental and social justice.

We are dedicated to producing beautiful books that combine outstanding literary content with design excellence.

Whit Press brings you the best of fiction, creative nonfiction, and poetry from diverse literary voices who do not have easy access to quality publication.

We publish stories of creative discovery, cultural insight, human experience, spiritual exploration, and more.

Whit Press and the Environment

Whit Press is a member of the Green Press Initiative. We are committed to eliminating the use of paper produced with endangered forest fiber.

Please visit our web site **www.WhitPress.org** for our other titles

THE WHEEL WRITING PROGRAM

The WHEEL Writing Program began in 1995 as a once a year project to collect and assemble writing and art from the Seattle homeless women's community for our yearly chapbook, which was to coincide with the **Homeless Women's Forum** that we began that year.

The **Homeless Women's Forum** is a major public event planned and carried out by homeless and formerly homeless women to speak on issues of homelessness that affect women, our victories of the past year, the goals we hope to accomplish in the next year, and how the rest of the community can help. It is a totally unique event.

The writing program expanded into workshops in the period immediately preceding the **Forum**, both to produce writing for the chapbook and to help women to work on their speeches for the **Forum**.

We also began increasingly to create written projects by group collaboration: the introductions to each of the poetry books, articles for *Real Change*, the *Seattle Post Intelligencer*, plus letters on various issues.

In 1999 we began **Women's Empowerment Center** activities — extended education and organizing activities, organized and administered by the women using the program. A writing workshop became part of the **Women's Empowerment Center**, by popular request.

One collaborative effort of the **WHEEL Women's Empowerment Center** was the **Thursday Breakfast and Education Project** at Antioch University, staffed by teachers from Antioch and other community volunteers. This program has frequently had guest workshop facilitators on everything from writing poetry, journaling, "writing your personal history," and bookmaking.

The **WHEEL Women's Empowerment Center** workshops have most often been facilitated by Anitra Freeman, who also facilitates a writing workshop for homeless and low-income adults called **StreetWrites**, at *Real Change* street newspaper. Writing by women of WHEEL has often been published in *Real Change* or in **StreetWrites** chapbooks, and writing by members of **StreetWrites** has often been published in WHEEL chapbooks.

Wherever or whatever writing workshops are held, they have a universal, empowering, effect. To create something from the heart, share it, and have others respond to you, is the essence both of building a community,, and of building a sense of self. As one of the poets of WHEEL, Cynthia Ozimek, expressed in the poem "Hammond": *But often / in stranger's eyes / we stumble upon our souls.* It is in the I/Thou relationship that we become individuals. It is in relating as unique and creative individuals that we make — and mend — our communities.

HOW TO HELP!

RESOLVE TO BE A COMMUNITY, homeless and housed, together. Homelessness is not just a loss of housing, it is a loss of community. Take an emotional inventory of your own negative attitudes toward homeless people. Do you involve them as part of your community? If negative perceptions hold you back, how can you deal with them?

Join WHEEL as we advocate for more shelter for homeless people until there is enough affordable housing for all. Or work to develop and support more homeless shelters in your local area. WHEEL has developed a How-To manual on starting shelters, and would be glad to consult with you.

Volunteer with WHEEL or your local homeless organizations. We need women who can share their gifts and talents.

Homeless or formerly homeless women, please join us or consider starting your own grassroots effort to improve lives and empower yourselves.

WHEEL always needs financial support. We work on a shoestring budget believing that money follows good work. We are a non-profit organizing effort; contributions are tax deductible.

For more information or other ways to help us, please contact us at:

WHEEL
Women's Housing, Equality and Enhancement League
P. O. Box 2548
Seattle, WA 98111-2458
(206) 956-0334